# Family Philanthropy

**Editor**
Barbara R Hauser

**Managing director**
Sian O'Neill

***Family Philanthropy***
**is published by**

Globe Law and Business Ltd
3 Mylor Close
Horsell
Woking
Surrey GU21 4DD
United Kingdom
Tel: +44 20 3745 4770
www.globelawandbusiness.com

Printed and bound by CPI Group (UK) Ltd, Croydon CR0 4YY, United Kingdom

*Family Philanthropy*

ISBN 9781787425187
EPUB ISBN 9781787425194
Adobe PDF ISBN 9781787425200

# Table of contents

# I. Introduction

**Barbara R Hauser**
Independent family adviser

This is a unique Special Report. It can be used in a number of ways. First, for families with a general interest in charitable causes, this is a rich resource. Each chapter addresses an intriguing topic. Philanthropy is a field of so many choices. The fun is in matching your family's or client's interest with an approach that fits them. As an outstanding resource for anyone, we are proud to present the views of some of the world's leading experts on a number of philanthropic topics.

We begin with a global perspective, from Rockefeller Philanthropy Advisors, and close with thoughts on the personal legacy one wants to leave for the next generation. This is also a very enjoyable Special Report to skip through. Each chapter can stand alone; together, they offer the broadest possible views, both globally and in terms of content. The authors wanted the information to be easy to access, but at the same time it is highly professional. The many charts and graphs add instant interest. Here is what you will find.

Rockefeller Philanthropy Advisors' Melissa Berman, Donzelina Barroso and Renee Karibi-Whyte begin with a global overview. They start by noting the recent increase in private philanthropy: "While some families have been engaged in philanthropy for decades (if not centuries), a diverse array of new philanthropists have recently entered the field." With fascinating global examples of several individuals, they highlight the rise in philanthropy. They see a universal human interest in philanthropy: "Families around the world share certain core reasons for engaging in philanthropy: a strong desire to give back to society, create social change, put values into action or address social inequality." They describe trends – of geographic wealth, ageing populations, social causes, collaborative giving, impact investing, even recent pandemic needs. With respect to impact, the authors note the growing involvement of the next generation and some of the related generational conflicts.

In sum, they conclude: "While family philanthropy is experiencing growth across the globe, it is also entering an era of rising expectations and rising challenges to legitimacy. It will be critical for family philanthropy in particular to show clearly how it is addressing inequity and global crises such as climate and healthcare disparities."

Next is a very practical – and unusual – chapter devoted to helping families engage in productive decision making about their philanthropy. Etienne Eichenberger of WISE and Małgorzata Kurak and Peter Vogel of IMD in Switzerland have recently written an entire book on this subject and share the key points of their research in this chapter. They suggest beginning with some key questions:

*"Good decision making is necessary for the management of giving, the involvement of the family and governance coordination across the entire system. Joined experience in philanthropy helps to create a shared legacy for the belief system that giving is part and parcel of life, which ultimately helps family members to become better humans and better decision makers."*

Etienne Eichenberger, Małgorzata Kurak and Peter Vogel (Chapter III)

- Which decisions would you like to take as a family and which governing body should be taking them (eg, family council, philanthropy committee, next-generation council, foundation board, foundation management, family office)?
- How will you be taking decisions as a family (eg, on projects, financial matters, strategic matters)?
- Which decisions do you delegate to other governance bodies within your family enterprise system (eg, family office, company board of directors)?
- How formal do you want your philanthropy governance to be?
- How can you progress while learning to improve your approach? Will your decision-making processes be linked to your data reports or benchmarks?

Based on extensive research, they offer a map to sort through these various decisions. They explain the three basic types of family decision making – unilateral decisions, board majority decisions and consensus decisions – and explore the advantages and disadvantages of each.

They conclude that: "Good decision making is necessary for the management of giving, the involvement of the family and governance coordination across the entire system. Joined experience in philanthropy helps to create a shared legacy for the belief system that giving is part and parcel of life, which ultimately helps family members to become better humans and better decision makers."

Once families have decided to embark on philanthropy, they will need to select a legal structure and method for their giving. Peter Cafferkey, of EVPA (the European Venture Philanthropy Association) and founder of Boncerto, and James Maloney of Farrer & Co set about demystifying the many choices. They list the factors to consider in selecting a jurisdiction, including tax treatments and general flexibility. Each jurisdiction may also have its own unique structures, including foundations, trusts and other forms.

They observe that in a growing number of cases, the family may choose to fund an operating 'charity' that does not comply with the tax definition of a 'charity'. This broader interest may lead to offshore structures as an option. In addition to the more traditional vehicles of philanthropy, new areas have developed in venture philanthropy, where families can apply their own business skills; in socially responsible investing, rather than merely giving out grants; and more recently in keeping with environmental, social and governance principles. They close by reassuring families that in this complex field, no one gets it right first time: "Part of our role is to help them be open to learning through trial and error in a controlled way, providing the safety nets through effective structuring to allow families to have an engaging, fulfilling and rewarding experience in philanthropy."

Their discussion of jurisdictional choices leads into Ineke Koele's argument that the Netherlands – where her tax and legal practice is based – is one of the best jurisdictions in Europe for charitable structures. She begins by citing the findings of the US-based Index of Philanthropic Freedom that: "The United States and the United Kingdom are well known for their sophisticated but highly regulated legal and tax framework for charities, but the Netherlands is widely regarded as the most liberal jurisdiction in the world for philanthropic organisations." She explains that there is very little oversight or regulation of charitable structures in the Netherlands. In addition, it is possible to create a foundation under Dutch law (with a small amount of oversight or regulation), even if none of the administration of the foundation takes place in the Netherlands. Her views are likely to spark interest among those with foundations in other jurisdictions. She walks through a number of issues to consider, such as including an exit strategy and using a combination of a Dutch foundation and a more limited structure in another jurisdiction. She closes with the observation that, if structured properly, Dutch resident foundations are completely transparent for Dutch tax purposes and offer a solid wealth planning structure without adding tax costs for an international family.

Also in relation to choosing a jurisdiction, the following chapter highlights several popular Caribbean locations. Appleby partner Vanessa Schrum compares three of the region's most respected jurisdictions, focusing primarily on the structuring options available in Bermuda, the British Virgin Islands (BVI) and the Cayman Islands. She notes that all of these jurisdictions are tax neutral and have stable governments, favourable but well-respected regulatory regimes and robust professional services industries. She includes a number of helpful tables to illustrate the various features of the charitable trusts and companies limited by guarantee which are used in Bermuda. In the BVI, a variety of trusts are used, including charitable trusts and 'purpose' trusts, although there are no charitable foundations. One of the more popular trusts in the BVI is a 'Vista trust', formed under the Virgin Islands Special Trusts Act 2003 and designed to allow trusts of BVI shares to be created where the trustee is disengaged from administrative and management responsibilities for the affairs of that BVI company (and by extension, any company held below that BVI company). The BVI also has companies limited by guarantee. Meanwhile, the charitable and philanthropic structures commonly found in Cayman include charitable trusts; the STAR regime (non-charitable purpose trusts); foundation companies; private family funds; companies; and unincorporated associations. Vanessa goes on to

*"The United States and the United Kingdom are well known for their sophisticated but highly regulated legal and tax framework for charities, but the Netherlands is widely regarded as the most liberal jurisdiction in the world for philanthropic organisations."*

Ineke A Koele (Chapter V)

describe the STAR trust, which is unique to Cayman and applies only where the trust instrument contains a declaration to that effect. It allows Cayman trusts to be created for philanthropic purposes which are outside of the scope of what would be considered charitable as a matter of Cayman Islands law.

Moving to the United States, Eileen Heisman, president and CEO of the National Philanthropic Trust, describes in some detail how 'donor-advised funds' (DAFs) work and why they have become so popular, even outside the United States. In her chapter, she gives a brief history of DAFs. Established in the 1930s at community charitable foundations, these are now the fastest-growing philanthropic vehicle in the United States. The number of DAFs exceeds private (charitable) foundations by nearly 10:1, although private foundations hold significantly more assets than DAFs. In the mid-1990s, financial institutions began launching their own charities to offer DAFs; they skyrocketed in popularity and today there are more than 850,000 individual DAF accounts in the United States, holding nearly $142 billion in charitable assets. The latter figure has increased by nearly 84% in the last five years alone. The main advantages of a DAF compared to a private (charitable) foundation are its flexibility, lower cost and streamlined accounting and record keeping. Complex regulations and some differing tax rules that apply to foundations also make DAFs more attractive. From a family point of view, the main drawback is that the family only advise the institution that sponsors the DAF as to where they would like grant distributions to be made; the sponsor has the final say. The trade-off of simplicity appears to be valuable. There is also encouragement to engage multiple family members and multiple generations in the role of fund advisers. Several family examples are included in this chapter, in addition to a number of useful charts.

An intriguing chapter comes next, as Kecia Barkawi, founder of a Swiss multi-family office, looks at the growing role of individual women in philanthropy around the world. She explores several important trends and begins by noting the large share of private wealth that is or will be in the hands of women:

> *The trend is global, and it is here to stay. In the United States, women are expected to control much of the $30 trillion that baby boomers will possess by 2030. In Asia, a new generation of women is transforming regional dynamics as more affluent, educated and empowered women come into the picture. And above-average growth of female wealth in Latin America, Eastern Europe, the Middle East and Africa is putting an increasing share of women in the driving seat of wealth decisions across the world.*

This growth in wealth is also a substantial driver for the future of philanthropy. In this context, Kecia looks at a number of examples set by some well-known women philanthropists – such as MacKenzie Scott and Melinda French Gates – and finds several distinctions in their patterns of giving. One is that women often make a point of giving 'early' during their life. In addition, there is an increase in spending down. Another is a pattern of collaborating and sharing with like-minded women, giving rise to a growing number of giving circles and donor networks globally. The examples of collaboration are a true inspiration for the future of giving and often support empowerment of women and girls. A further trend is to give strategically by setting clear goals and evaluating the philanthropic impact through grantmaking and also, increasingly, investment.

In Germany, Christian von Oertzen and Tanja Schienke-Ohletz of Flick Gocke Schaumburg take a look at families that support major cultural institutions. They focus on some major philanthropic purposes involving art and culture of all types, and ideally as family endeavours. They suggest that a family should begin by asking what they want to accomplish and why. For example, if the family want to support arts and culture, they should consider what kind of cultural purposes they want to foster – for example, a museum or a certain art style. Are there defined family values – for example, should the family's art collection be made available to the general public or should scientific research be undertaken? Which resources can the family use? It is also crucial to determine whether the endeavour is important only to the senior generation or whether multiple generations will be involved. Instead of creating a new museum, an alternative strategy is to negotiate a loan agreement with a museum or to support an organisation through a 'friends of' relationship. These agreements are explored in detail and diagrams of the various choices are included. The authors close with the hope that future generations will continue their involvement in family charities. To this end, it will be important for the older generation to liaise with the younger generation to reach a compromise of ideas. The latter will also have to be onboarded in the charity or in other philanthropic activities, so that they are prepared to take over important roles one day.

The closing chapter, by Swiss-based adviser Diana Chambers, begins by asking the big final question: how would you like to be remembered? What will your philanthropic legacy be? The chapter starts with an apt quote from anthropologist and primatologist Jane Goodall: "You cannot get through a single day without having an impact on the world around you. What you do makes a difference, and you have to decide what kind of difference you want to make." Diana thinks systemically; so this Special Report, which began with a look at global trends in giving, ends with a societal and global perspective on legacy. She invites us to determine what the world needs most at this critical juncture in history and how we can positively impact cultural systems, with a fundamental dimension being to understand the impact of trauma on individuals and societies. She presents five themes for consideration: what it means to be philanthropic; appreciating your legacy to date; considering when to shape your legacy; including in your legacy what the world needs now; and the impact of your legacy on your descendants.

Her closing thoughts are to slow down, ask the right questions and allow the answers to be revealed. Asking the right questions is more important than having all the answers. With a contemplative approach, she is convinced that the answers will appear.

# II. Family philanthropy: an overview of global giving and trends

**Donzelina Barroso**
**Melissa A Berman**
**Renee Karibi-Whyte**
Rockefeller Philanthropy Advisors

**1. Introduction**

Family philanthropy around the globe is a dynamic and important part of the overall social change landscape. Reflective of local cultures and values, it encompasses charitable efforts of all sizes and is expressed through a growing range of vehicles and approaches.

Family philanthropy can include anything from the joint efforts of a small family unit, such as siblings or a couple, all the way to initiatives of a large extended multi-generational family, including cousins and spouses. It can mean a philanthropic effort with no external staff, run by the family itself; one with professional staff and a less engaged family; and anything in between. Family philanthropy is sometimes very localised, centring on a community; or can be focused on an issue that involves cross-border giving.

In terms of structure, family philanthropy may be formalised as a grant-making foundation; an operating foundation that runs its own programmes; a charitable trust; family investments focused on impact; a donor-advised fund (DAF); or simply out-of-pocket giving. It may operate as an independent organisation or, in the case of a DAF or other charitable fund, may be held under the auspices of a charitable umbrella organisation. Tax considerations, ease of use and flexibility can be critical factors in determining the vehicle(s) of choice.

While some families have been engaged in philanthropy for decades (if not centuries), a diverse array of new philanthropists have recently entered the field, in part due to a steady increase in the number of global wealth holders over the past two decades. Living donors such as Jack Ma (China), MacKenzie Scott and Dan Jewett (United States), the Carasso family (France and Spain) and the Marinho family (Brazil) bring with them a range of professional experiences, creativity, questions, enthusiasm and personal engagement. A recent comprehensive global study of the sector as a whole, *Global Philanthropy Report: Perspectives on the Global Foundation Sector* by Paula Johnson, indicates that a significant number of the nearly 80,000 foundations in its cohort (44%) were created after the year 2000.[1] This trend is similar, though less pronounced, when viewing family philanthropy specifically. A recent Rockefeller Philanthropy Advisors (RPA) survey indicated that 28% of the 200-plus responding global families began engaging in philanthropy during or after the year 2000.[2]

**2. Motivations and causes**

Why do families become involved in significant philanthropy? The reasons can be as varied as the families themselves. For some families, philanthropy is about making one person's vision come to life; for others, it is an opportunity to work towards common family values and goals. With multi-generational families, a common philanthropic project can also be a means to encourage family unity or reinforce family business values. For others, family philanthropy offers an opportunity for visibility and recognition.

Regardless of the initial impetus or differences in structure, size and topics addressed, families around the world share certain core reasons for engaging in philanthropy: a strong desire to give back to society, create social change, put values into action or address social inequality.[3]

In terms of areas of philanthropic interest, families tend to focus on education, health and human services/social welfare across the globe. In the RPA survey of family wealth holders, philanthropy portfolios were weighted most heavily towards education (an average of 29%), health (14%) and social justice, social and human services (13% combined).[4] This has been consistent over time and across the wealth spectrum. Many donors understand education as a lever to escape poverty and reduce social inequality, and thus there is a strong focus on giving across cultures. Health is perceived as a necessary baseline for living a productive, enriching life; and for many families, personal experience can influence a donor to give in support of a particular medical cause. Much of giving globally is also directed towards providing direct support to persons in need, and thus a significant portion of global giving is classified under human services.

**Figure 1. Why are you giving?**

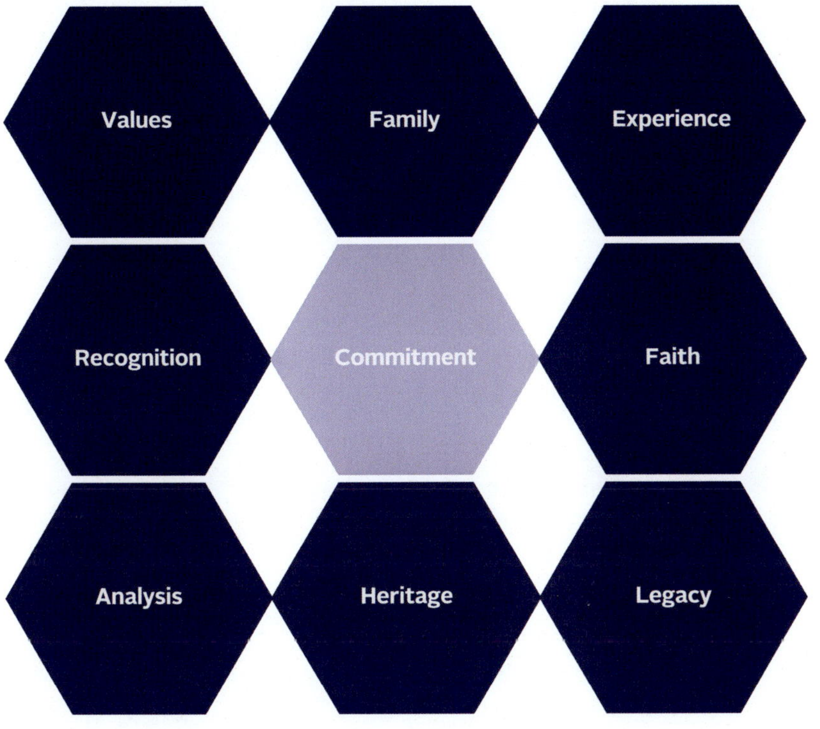


*Regardless of geography, the core values that bring donors to the table are consistent. This partial list shows some of the commonly expressed reasons for engaging in a philanthropic endeavour.*

*Source: Rockefeller Philanthropy Advisors.*

**Figure 2. Causes supported as percentage of portfolio**

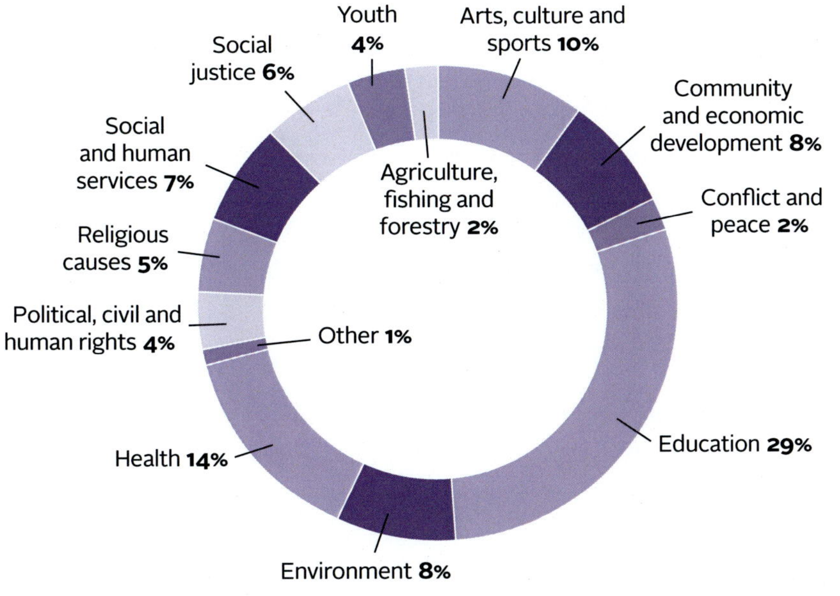


*Source: Rockefeller Philanthropy Advisors and Campden Wealth,* "Global Trends and Strategic Time Horizons in Family Philanthropy" *(2020).*

Data on global giving to the Sustainable Development Goals (SDGs) from 2016 to the present reflects these findings. Of the $216.5 billion committed during that period, the vast majority was directed to SDG 4, Quality Education, which received $87.4 billion; and SDG 3, Good Health and Wellbeing, which received $69.1 billion. The next-most funded SDG – SDG 16, Peace, Justice & Strong Institutions – received $22.4 billion.[5] While education and health are broad categories that include a very wide range of options, other causes such as environment/climate are emerging as strong areas of interest, particularly among younger donors.

### 3. Giving patterns

Wealth trends are generally good indicators of where philanthropy will grow, as strong philanthropic and non-profit infrastructure is typically associated with higher-income countries.[6] As economies develop and new wealth and disposable income emerge, individuals, families and companies are more likely to engage in giving.

In the past 15 years, there has been a steady increase across categories of wealth globally. The ultra-high-net-worth (UHNW) population, with $30 million-plus in net worth, has grown by 105% over that timeframe, from 142,420 to 291,470 individuals. The very high-net-worth population, with between $5 million and $30 million in net worth, has also more than doubled, to 2.67 million.[7]

#### 3.1 Geographic trends

In terms of representation of family foundations as a percentage of all foundations by region, Africa has the highest concentration, with families representing 36% of philanthropies. At the other end is the Asia-Pacific region, where families represent only 1% of all philanthropies. In between are North America (4%); Europe (10%); the Middle East (12%) and Latin America (17%).[8] Despite the difference in regional percentages represented by family philanthropy, foundations and assets historically have been and still remain heavily concentrated in the United States and Europe.

There are signs, however, that there will be a much higher representation from Asia within the next decade. Much new economic growth is driven by Asia, which recently surpassed Europe in numbers of UHNW individuals (UHNWIs). During the past decade, 60% of the top 10 fastest-growing global wealth markets have been in East or South Asia.[9] China in particular has an outsized number of emerging UHNWIs: of the top 30 global cities with the fastest growth, 26 are located in China.[10] Further, when looking at number of foundations created since 2000, most other regions have maintained steady growth or shown a decline in numbers, while Asia has experienced consistent and steep growth.[11]

*"Wealth trends are generally good indicators of where philanthropy will grow, as strong philanthropic and non-profit infrastructure is typically associated with higher-income countries."*

**3.2 Ageing population**

Even beyond geographic changes, there are signals that more families are engaging in philanthropy. Among wealth holders, increased interest in philanthropy correlates with increased age. Of respondents surveyed by Wealth-X, nearly half of those aged 70-plus in the UHNW category listed philanthropy as a top interest/passion; while in the 50-70 age group category, that number fell to 35.4%. In the under-50 group, only 25.9% listed philanthropy as a primary interest.[12] This would indicate that as middle-aged next-generation inheritors/donors grow older, they will become more active in their giving.

Another indicator is found in the Annual Wealth Report published by UK-based luxury real estate consultancy Knight Frank. In a survey of over 620 global private bankers/wealth advisers with assets under management of over $3.3 trillion across geographies, at least 60% stated that their clients were increasing their philanthropic activities.[13]

**3.3 Philanthropic flows**

Families often give within their own communities and many support place-based philanthropy. Additionally, different regions tend to have families that are more or less involved in cross-border giving, as philanthropic flows reflect global need. RPA's family philanthropy survey found that the majority of families in the Asia-Pacific region

(89%) and North America (78%) fund activities in their own region; while only 38% of Europeans give to causes primarily in Europe.[14] Europeans reported being the most likely to give to initiatives in Africa at 18%, compared to 7% for North Americans and 4% in Asia-Pacific.[15] However, Africa nonetheless ranked at the top of the externally focused funds for North Americans, with 6% going to Asia, 4% to the Middle East, 3% to Europe and 2% to Latin America. Overall, Europe and North America showed net negative philanthropic inflows in this survey, with 50% of responding families being located there and only 39% of global respondents supporting initiatives in North America. Similarly, only 13% of global respondents funded initiatives in Europe, despite 25% of all respondents being based in Europe. For example, Asia and Africa have outsized needs when it comes to achieving the SDGs and thus have received significant flows of capital. Further, as their own philanthropic cohorts develop, we expect to see the portion of in-country flows to increase.

### 3.4 The Giving Pledge

The Giving Pledge, which was started in 2010 by Bill and Melinda Gates and Warren Buffett, is closely related to time-limited philanthropy. It was created with the idea to "help shift the social norms of philanthropy among the world's wealthiest people and

*"Philanthropy among families is responsive to external factors and to new approaches. Families often have deep ties to the places they fund and direct on-the-ground knowledge, and can thus adapt their approaches as needed."*

inspire people to give more, establish their giving plans sooner, and give in smarter ways".[16] Those with a net worth of $1 billion or more can join and publicly commit to giving a majority of their wealth to philanthropy, during their lifetime or in their wills. The network continues to grow and currently includes over 200 individuals or families representing 25 countries. Like philanthropists in a collaborative, Giving Pledge members learn from each other and come together to share lessons learned and exchange experiences in large-scale, high-impact philanthropy.

**4. Evolving approaches to family philanthropy**

Philanthropy among families is responsive to external factors and to new approaches. Families often have deep ties to the places they fund and direct on-the-ground knowledge, and can thus adapt their approaches as needed. The trends to which families respond will impact not only the types of activities in which they engage, but also how those donors think about the structure of their philanthropies and the expectations of the trusted advisers who assist them. Younger generations in particular – some not yet inheritors – are questioning the status quo not only of their family's philanthropy, but also aspects of asset and business management. Issues such as climate and inequality are becoming more prominent; and the urgency of the moment, accompanied by increased scrutiny of the sector across the globe, demands new responses.

**4.1 The evolving social compact**

As wealth has become more concentrated and income inequality has increased, there has been renewed attention on the influence that private resources may wield over societal issues that are commonly considered the purview of governments (public health policy, education, social services). While the focus has been on, for example, the Gates Foundation, which has the scale to shift public health and other policies of independent nations, much smaller philanthropies working locally may also be open to critique. This criticism can range from questioning the causes or issues that the family chooses to support to the way in which they provide that support. For much of the public at large, the operations and decision-making processes of foundations appear opaque, and conspiracy theories abound about the intentions of donors and wealthy global families in particular. And in the case of funds coming from outside the community, region or country, there is sometimes even more concern over foreign influence.

Foundations in fact can operate very independently, without much oversight other than sticking to definitions of 'charitable activity' and financial oversight related to the handling of the financial resources dedicated to that activity. As these issues have come to the fore over the past several years, more and more philanthropic families are shifting how they approach their social compact with society. These changes, which are designed to help improve trust and help the public to understand the value of philanthropy, include:

- taking steps to enhance accountability and perceived legitimacy by increasing transparency about a philanthropy's purpose, processes and approaches (eg, including investment of the endowment); and
- engaging even more deeply with grantees and communities served by including them in decision-making and governance structures.[17]

*Giving to pandemic-related causes has far surpassed that of giving to other disaster relief efforts. Across the spectrum of developing and developed nations, immediate needs – food, health and job security issues – took precedence, putting other concerns on hold. Market volatility has harmed some foundations' ability to engage, particularly for those that make annual allocations to philanthropy from a business; and has helped others, including those from the technology fields that are keeping us all connected at this time.*

**4.2 Systems change perspective**

The global COVID-19 pandemic has had an unquestionable impact on philanthropic practice, due in large part to the unprecedented need for emergency relief, much of which fell outside usual giving strategies and above usual budgetary capacities. Family foundations and other philanthropists stepped in to fill a yawning gap, reducing restrictions on how the money is used and shortening processes for getting funding to service organisations. With the ongoing effects of the pandemic (the World Bank estimated that by the end of 2021, COVID-19 might have pushed as many as 150 million persons back into extreme poverty),[18] many families have re-examined their strategies and values. Some have been energised to think about how they define impact, and to re-examine practices related to relationships with grantees and other partners.

**Figure 3. Philanthropic funding for COVID-19 compared with recent disasters**

Based on data, in US dollars, collected for roughly six months following each disaster.

*Source: Candid and the Center for Disaster Philanthropy,* "Philanthropy and COVID-19 in the first half of 2020" *(2020).*

**Figure 4. The iceberg model**

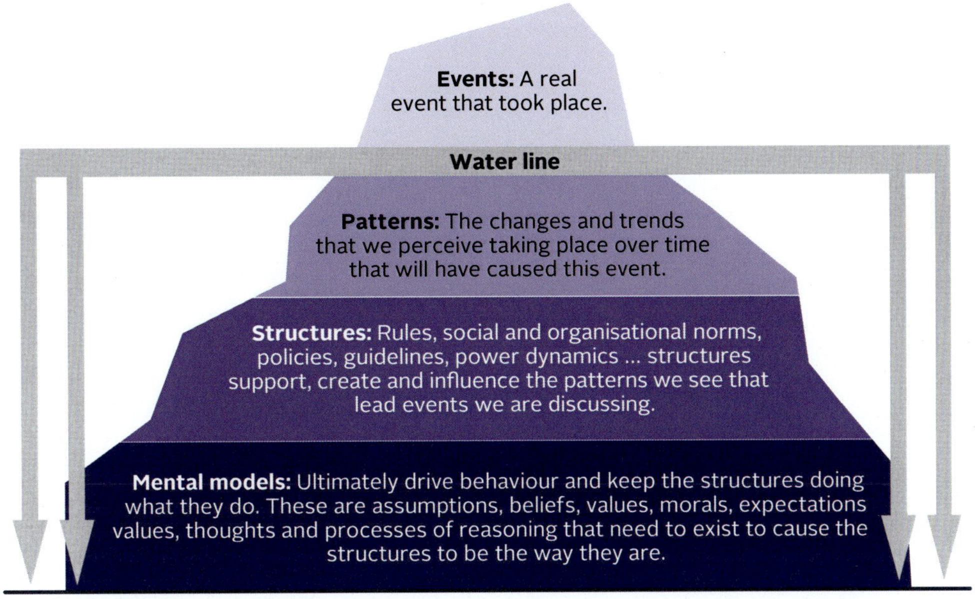


*Source: Rockefeller Philanthropy Advisors,* "Seeing, Facilitating, and Assessing Systems Change: Learnings from the Scaling Solutions toward Shifting Systems Initiative" *(2020). The iceberg model of culture was developed by anthropologist Michael T Hall in the 1970s and has been adapted and adopted by those studying systems change.*

A recent report by Candid and the Center for Disaster Philanthropy[19] puts the level of COVID-19 funding in perspective: while previous disasters mobilised hundreds of millions of dollars, the COVID-19 response has been in the billions.

Increased recognition of systemic racial inequities, particularly in the United States, along with other persistent inequities around the globe, has also increased interest among families and other donors in an approach focused on systems change, or using giving to find solutions that address the underlying root causes of social, economic and environmental problems. This type of philanthropic approach requires a longer-term view and a different type of philanthropic strategy.

One helpful metaphor that many funders use is an iceberg: events such as COVID-19 are the visible parts – above the waterline – of a complex problem; while below the surface are issues about access, rights and trust.

Developing a vaccine is what policy planners often call a 'tame' problem: society largely agrees on what a vaccine is and how its effectiveness is measured. When it comes to how this work should be funded, how vaccines should be distributed and whether vaccines should be mandated, we are in the realm of 'wicked problems' – those for which there is no clear definition or agreement on an appropriate solution.[20]

Wicked problems involve systems change. For example, getting vaccines to people in many countries will depend on changing the entire public health system, which is itself connected to countries' economic wellbeing. From RPA's perspective, no single funder can shift an entire system; but we recommend that donors understand the larger systems context in which a discrete problem exists. Funders can then choose to focus their philanthropy on one of the following levels:

- incremental – improving outcomes within existing rules and norms;
- reform – changing rules and norms so that new types of actions become increasingly prevalent; and
- transformation – creating previously unimagined ways of tackling problems.[21]

### 4.3 Rights and equity lens

Many family philanthropies around the world are long-time supporters of human rights. Traditionally, this funding has been framed around civil and political rights, as enshrined in the United Nations Universal Declaration of Human Rights, adopted in 1948.[22] In recent years, many families have started giving attention to economic, environmental, social and cultural rights.[23] This means that many donors now ask how programmes in all their funding areas (eg, education, health, poverty reduction) strengthen the rights and opportunities of the disadvantaged.

Family philanthropies are also exploring ways to ensure that their funding goes to local organisations, led by leaders who represent the communities most directly affected. They may also impose fewer requirements for the use of their funding, convinced that charitable organisations in the midst of a problem have the best understanding of how to make change happen. As noted, the quick, generous and unrestricted support that the COVID-19 pandemic inspired has led many individuals and family donors to be more inclined to trust their non-profit partners.

### 4.4 Collaborative giving

As the landscape of philanthropy evolves, it is increasingly evident that the future of systems change requires not only larger pools of funding, but also more combined willpower and expertise. For this reason, more family philanthropies are exploring opportunities to partner with other donors to achieve greater impact. These joint efforts, referred to as 'collaboratives', can be an avenue to developing deeper expertise by leveraging the wisdom and experience of the partners. Moreover, interacting with others in this way can encourage more thoughtful decision making. When a foundation acts alone, it may be more likely to give without an overall strategy or rubric for decision making. The

**Figure 5. Spectrum of collaborative giving**

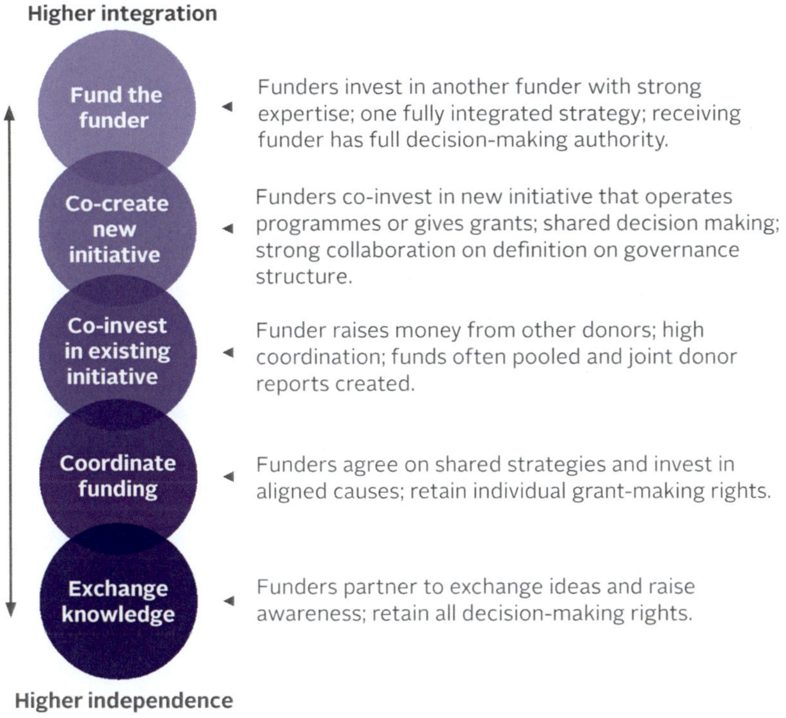


*Source: Rockefeller Philanthropy Advisors Philanthropy Roadmap,* "Collaborative Giving" *(2017).*

*The spectrum of collaborative giving includes everything from the exchange of ideas to pooled funds with one fully integrated strategy and less donor decision-making autonomy.*

act of reaching agreement with others to define a process, goals and strategy in and of itself can be educational, while creating the satisfaction of an integrated giving strategy that aligns with a donor's personal values, as well as those of the group. Thus, even experienced donors can benefit from tapping into the skillsets and expertise of their peers. With access to the wisdom of other donors, a wider network of advisers and other shared resources, collaboration can mitigate the risks of engaging in an effort alone or duplicating efforts while still on a learning curve.

When funds are pooled for longer-term or larger gifts, grantees may also be freed from excessive reporting duties and will enjoy the security of knowing that their big visions are supported by a more substantial flow of capital, helping them to grow their initiatives without the uncertainty of consistently applying for smaller, shorter-term funding. This, too, increases the impact of the funds provided.[24]

### 4.5 Impact investing

Originally coined in 2007 at a convening hosted by the Rockefeller Foundation's Bellagio Center in northern Italy, the term 'impact investing' describes investments that generate social and/or environmental benefits while delivering a financial return. This is another tool in the toolbox of family philanthropy and it has grown

*RPA's* Impact Investing Handbook *helps donors and families interested in taking a more 'all assets' approach to their philanthropy to define key components that will help form a cohesive strategy.*

**Figure 6. Impact Investing Roadmap**

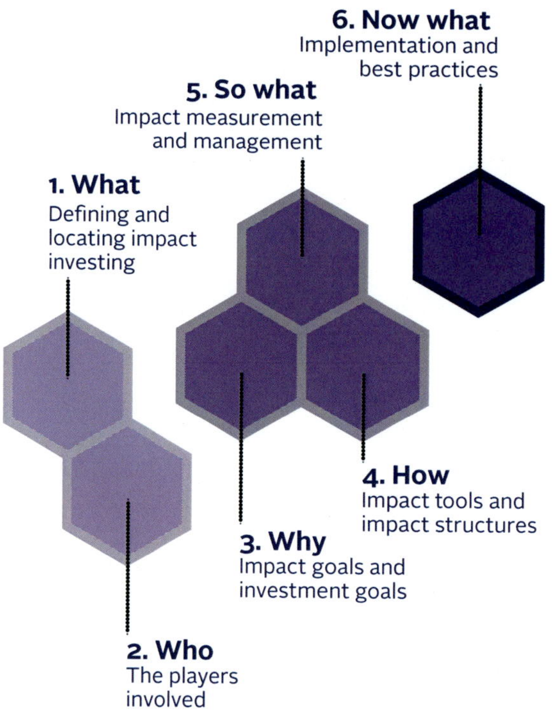


*Source: Steven Godeke and Patrick Briaud,* Impact Investing Handbook: An Implementation Guide for Practitioners *(Rockefeller Philanthropy Advisors, 2020).*

tremendously in the years since. Just over a decade later, in 2020, the impact investing market touched $715 billion in assets under management, according to the Global Impact Investing Network.[25]

Among the various investor segments, private investors and family offices – especially UHNWIs – are driving the impact investing market, given the flexibility, long-term orientation and broader valuation prism of private 'patient' capital. It is no surprise that one-quarter of family offices are involved in impact investing today and over one-third expect to grow their impact investing budget to over 24% of their portfolio by 2024.[26] Even retrospectively, 81% of family offices said that their impact investments met or exceeded their expectations.[27]

The next generation of wealth inheritors is especially and increasingly inclined to create a positive social impact through their investments, given that they tend to be more environmentally conscientious and concerned about social justice. We increasingly see this lens applied to family foundation endowments as well.

**5. Strategic time horizons for giving**

Family and other types of philanthropies are increasingly intentional about their giving timelines. Whether the timeframe decided upon is 'in perpetuity' or limited, the act of pre-determining what it will be is referred to as 'setting a strategic time horizon'. More than ever before, foundations – including family foundations – are now created with a specific end date in mind; or, in the case of in-perpetuity foundations, switching to a 'giving while living' or defined end point model.[28]

Time-limited philanthropy falls into one of several models:

- those with a defined end date, such as a specific day, month or year;
- those that have an end date triggered by an event – for example, five years after the death of the founder; and
- those that fall into the 'giving while living' category, made famous by Chuck Feeney, founder of Atlantic Philanthropies, which recently completed its planned spend-down.

Along with the in-perpetuity model, each of these has advantages depending on the criteria that are most important to the family.

Those families that adopt a time-limited philanthropic horizon do so for one or more of several reasons. One of the top reasons, expressed by nearly one-third (30%) of respondents to an RPA family philanthropy survey, is the founders' desire to see the impact on

**Figure 7. Strategic time horizons: key considerations**

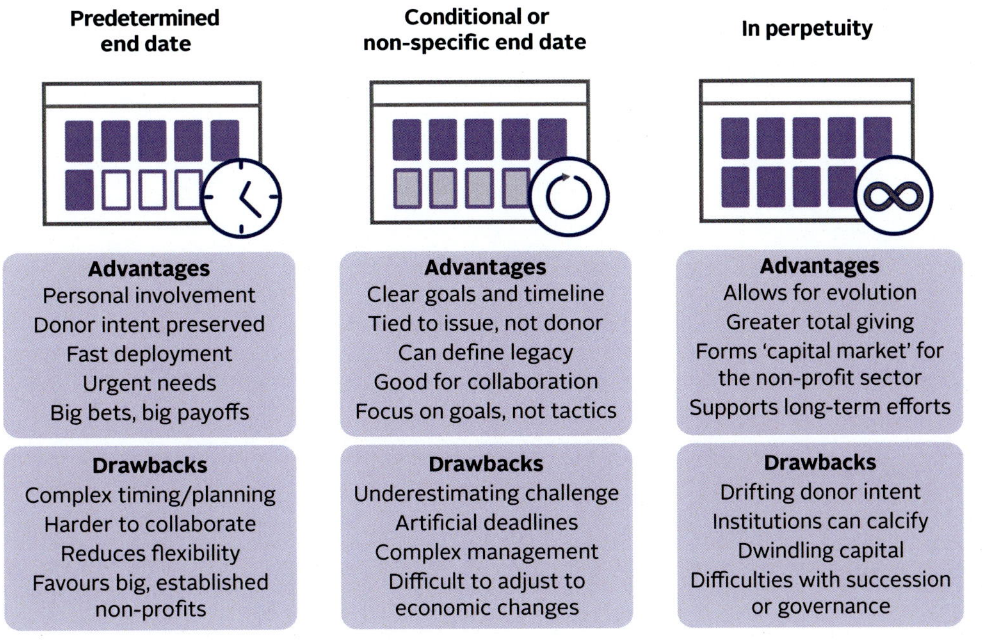


*Source: Rockefeller Philanthropy Advisors Philanthropy Roadmap,* "Strategic Time Horizons in Philanthropy: Key Trends and Considerations" *(2021).*

beneficiaries during their lifetimes. The second-most expressed reason was that a limited timeframe allowed them to make a greater impact by narrowing their focus (23% of responding families). When those engaged in time-limited giving were asked to indicate the "best reasons to engage in time-limited philanthropy", 56% reported that it provides a clear focus for donating; 46% believed it ensures that the "problems of today" are addressed; and 38% said that "it is the best strategy to ensure that families' wishes are met".

Family philanthropies that choose an in-perpetuity approach overwhelmingly (71%) do so based on the belief it can enable sustained and long-term support to address persistent challenges. Other reasons include its role in strengthening a family's purpose and values (56%); and its impact on beneficiaries across multiple generations (41%). In the words of one anonymous respondent: "[T]here will always be something to do when it comes to children's health. We will be best prepared to tackle new challenges if we are around and viable in the long term."

**6. Next-generation involvement**
The growing impact of the next generation of wealth holders will be felt in philanthropy for years to come. Not only do they tend to have

*"The next generation's involvement in philanthropy can be a rich source of fresh ideas. However, it can also be a source of tension, stemming, for example, from differing visions about the purpose of the organisation."*

different interest areas from prior generations; they are also more apt to embrace different methods for giving, often including technology-based approaches. And while next-generation involvement in giving is not new in philanthropy, RPA has observed an emerging trend of some young family members taking a strong stance on issues relating not only to family wealth, but also to the entire system that enabled that wealth creation and the increased concentration we are witnessing. Many of these next-generation members – some of whom have not yet become engaged in family business, investments or philanthropy – hold social inequality as a main focus and see redistribution as a goal, beyond simply with philanthropic capital. This will surely influence investment strategies for their resources, as well as giving plans.

Because of this desire to make an impact, next-generation involvement in philanthropy is very high. RPA's 2020 survey of philanthropic families found next-generation involvement in 81% of responding families, almost evenly split between being "actively involved" (42%) or "somewhat involved" (39%). The level of activity was relatively consistent across regions globally.

The roles most often played by the next generation in their families' philanthropy included serving on boards (45%), conducting site visits (28%) and developing grants (24%). In terms of regional differences, next-generation representatives were more likely to participate in board service in the United States (45%) and Europe (43%) than in Asia-Pacific (37%). They were also more likely to conduct site visits and play an active role in grant making in the United States (38% and 32% respectively) than in either Europe (18% and 14% respectively) or Asia-Pacific (24% for both categories). Conversely, next-generation representatives in Asia-Pacific were more often included in key operational decisions (34%) than their counterparts in the United States (11%) and Europe (14%).

The next generation's involvement in philanthropy can be a rich source of fresh ideas. However, it can also be a source of tension, stemming, for example, from differing visions about the purpose of the organisation. Asked how they would respond if the next generation proposed a change to the existing philanthropic strategy, respondents on the whole indicated that they would take a collaborative approach. The majority of the philanthropists surveyed (76%) stated that they would listen to the next generation's plans before making an informed decision. Respondents in Asia-Pacific were more likely to select this option (83%) than those in Europe (69%) or the United States (66%). The second most popular approach was to work on reaching a compromise that would take the next generation's views into account (29% globally).

Here again, those in Asia-Pacific were most likely to engage in this manner (33%), followed by Europe (24%) and the United States (16 %). Some respondents, however, stated that the philanthropic organisation would likely continue with its existing strategy (18%) or give the next generation funds to set up a separate organisation (18%). These findings remain relatively consistent across the time-limited and in-perpetuity models, with listening to the next generation's plans prior to making a decision, working to reach a compromise and continuing with the existing strategy the top approaches in each case. The only subtle differences were that time-limited respondents were somewhat less likely than their in-perpetuity peers to select the first option.

**7. Decision-making structures in family philanthropy**

As families get more involved in or adjust their approach to philanthropy, they often look anew at decision-making structures within their organisations. For most family philanthropy, the head of the family is a key decision maker, followed by other family members and trustees.[29] Larger, in-perpetuity family foundations are slightly less likely to have the head of the family as the key decision maker (71% versus 55%), as a broader cohort such as the board may have more decision-making power. In terms of day-to-day management and operations, family members are equally as likely as not to exercise operational control and perform day-to-day management of the foundation.

In 27% of the cases, day-to-day management was entrusted to dedicated philanthropic staff and in 21% to (non-family) family office staff. Regional analysis showed similar distributions of everyday managerial responsibilities. However, while 21% of participants in the United States indicated that such responsibilities were held by dedicated philanthropic staff or external advisers, 38% in Europe said the same.[30]

**8. Assessing impact**

Donors often struggle to understand the true impact of their giving. The complexity of social problems tackled by philanthropy means that progress may be slow and difficult to define.

There is a broad spectrum of assessment tools. At one end is simple goals versus outcomes reporting, in which grantees report how they performed in relation to predetermined and clearly defined goals. At the other end are more complex designs that measure target populations against comparable populations who did not receive the same programme or return on investment methods, which seek to quantify the results in relation to funds invested. The more complex a method becomes, the more time and resources that it will take to implement.[31]

There are three main reasons for assessing the results of philanthropic investments:

- Accountability: Assessment helps donors to understand whether their partners (grantees) have used funds in the way that was agreed. If scholarships were funded, was the money distributed to the appropriate number of scholarship students, for example?
- Decision making: Assessment can provide context-informed choices – did one group have better results than another providing similar services? Or did a grant fall short because the organisation may have needed additional support? In this case the data can help donors to understand how they can be more effective partners to organisations working in their area of interest.
- Proof of concept: Assessment can provide evidence that a particular intervention was successful, and thus offer evidence to be shared with others to encourage replication.

Assessment can be most effective when incorporated into early discussions about philanthropic strategy, so that methods selected are relevant to the complexity of the programmes supported, and also provide valuable, actionable information. As measurement may encompass several goals, RPA recommends that donors think carefully about what they hope to achieve. In this way, they can also define what is most important for them to understand about how their resources are applied, and can thus select an appropriate method. This process of reflection and planning is also applicable to family philanthropies running their own programmes.

Questions to consider include the following:

- What problem are you trying to solve?
- How do you think change will happen?
- How long will it take?
- How much money will it take?
- What will success look like?
- What will be the signs of progress on the way?
- How do the groups directly addressing these problems answer these questions?
- Who else is working on this and what assessment tools are they using?
- How much time and money are you willing to invest in assessment?

While the quality of the assessment ultimately depends on factors including the method adopted, the implementation of the assessment method and the amount of money invested, it is important for donors to be realistic about how far their resources will go when making a choice. Current thinking in the field ascribes a contributory rather than attributional role to most giving.

Likewise, it is equally important to be realistic about the capacity of the groups being supported to produce the reports and data requested. Donors often find that they may need to help build the internal capacity of their grantees or even provide additional resources (technical assistance or financial resources) to enable them to collect data. For that reason, collecting the right level of data and matching the assessment method to a programme's complexity and the grantee's capacity are also important elements in overall philanthropic strategy.

**Figure 8. Understanding what measurement can do**

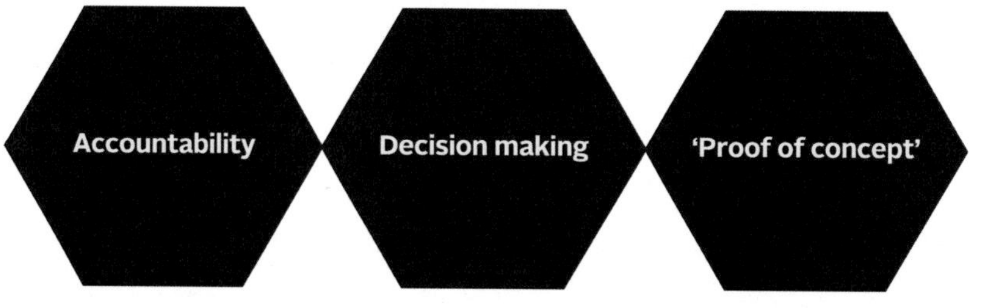


*Source: Rockefeller Philanthropy Advisors Philanthropy Roadmap,* "Assessing Impact" *(2017).*

## 9. Conclusion

While family philanthropy is experiencing growth across the globe, it is also entering an era of rising expectations and rising challenges to legitimacy. It will be critical for family philanthropy in particular to show clearly how it is addressing inequity and global crises such as climate and healthcare disparities.

## Notes

1 Paula Johnson, *Global Philanthropy Report: Perspectives on the Global Foundation Sector* (Harvard Kennedy School, 2018), https://cpl.hks.harvard.edu/files/cpl/files/global_philanthropy_report_final_april_2018.pdf?m=1524750312.
2 Rockefeller Philanthropy Advisors and Campden Wealth, *Global Trends and Strategic Time Horizons in Family Philanthropy 2020*, www.rockpa.org/wp-content/uploads/2020/01/Global-Trends-and-Strategic-Time-Horizons-in-Family-Philanthropy_FINAL.pdf.
3 Of the 201 private/family philanthropists from 28 countries surveyed, each with a net wealth of at least $100 million, 75% rated giving back to society as their top reason for giving, followed by an interest in creating social change (55%), putting values into action (50%) and addressing social inequality (47%). See Rockefeller Philanthropy Advisors (n 2).
4 Rockefeller Philanthropy Advisors (n 2) 14.
5 Global data compiled by Candid is based on data submitted to the organisation by donors as well as global data interpreted through algorithms to indicate SDG alignment. Data is skewed towards the United States, where giving is detailed on 990 tax forms, but global data is included, and Candid refines its capabilities over time. See SDG Funders, https://sdgfunders.org/home/.
6 Paula Johnson (n 1).

7 Wealth-X, *A Decade of Wealth: A Review of the Past 10 Years in Wealth and a Look Forward to the Decade to Come* (May 2020), www.wealthx.com/report/decade-of-wealth/.
8 Paula Johnson (n 1) 15.
9 Wealth-X (n 7).
10 *Ibid.*
11 Paula Johnson (n 1).
12 Given that the survey included a majority of self-made wealth holders, this might be explained in part by the UHNWIs 'slowing down' after achieving success in their business endeavours. The respondent breakdown was 68% self-made, 24% inherited/self-made and 8% inherited. See Wealth *Ultra Wealthy Population Analysis: The World Ultra Wealth Report* (September 2019), www.wealthx.com/report/world-ultra-wealth-report-2019/.
13 Knight Frank, *The Wealth Report 2020* (May 2020), www.knightfrank.com/wealthreport.
14 Rockefeller Philanthropy Advisors (n 2), 16.
15 This survey had a statistically insignificant response rate from families in Africa, so it was not possible to make conclusions regarding flows from that region.
16 Giving Pledge, https://givingpledge.org/About.aspx.
17 Rockefeller Philanthropy Advisors, *Social Compact in a Changing World: How Philanthropies Are Grappling with Growing Scrutiny and Critique* (September 2019), www.rockpa.org/wp-content/uploads/2019/09/Social-Compact-in-a-Changing-World.pdf.
18 The World Bank, "COVID19 to Add as Many as 150 Million Extreme Poor by 2021" (7 October 2020), www.worldbank.org/en/news/press-release/2020/10/07/covid-19-to-add-as-many-as-150-million-extreme-poor-by-2021.
19 Candid and the Center for Disaster Philanthropy, *Philanthropy and COVID-19 in the first half of 2020* (2020), www.issuelab.org/resources/37232/37232.pdf.
20 Horst WJ Rittel and Melvin M Webber, "Dilemmas in a General Theory of Planning," (1973) 4 *Policy Sciences* 155.
21 Rockefeller Philanthropy Advisors, *Scaling Solutions Toward Shifting Systems: Seeing, Facilitating, and Assessing Systems Change* (2020), www.rockpa.org/wp-content/uploads/2020/11/11-17-RockPA-Scaling-Solutions-03-Report-LowRes.pdf.
22 www.un.org/en/about-us/universal-declaration-of-human-rights.
23 Victoria Ibezim-Ohaeri, "Human rights: a bread and butter issue?" *Alliance* (3 September 2019) 48.
24 Rockefeller Philanthropy Advisors *Collaborative Giving*, www.rockpa.org/wp-content/uploads/2017/12/RPA_PRM_Collaborative_Giving_FINAL-web.pdf.
25 Dean Hand, Hannah Dithrich, Sophia Sunderji and Noshin Nova, *2020 Annual Impact Investor Survey* (Global Impact Investing Network, 11 June 2020), https://thegiin.org/research/publication/impinv-survey-2020.
26 UBS, *Global Family Office Report 2019* (Campden Research, 2019), www.ubs.com/global/en/wealth-management/uhnw/global-family-office-report/global-family-office-report-2019.html.
27 *Ibid.*
28 See Rockefeller Philanthropy Advisors (n 2) for a full exploration of strategic time horizons in giving.
29 Rockefeller Philanthropy Advisors (n 2). This is particularly so in Europe (74%) and Asia-Pacific (62%), as opposed to the United States (54%). Other family members were more likely to be key decision makers in the United States (65%), with a significantly lower likelihood in Asia-Pacific (31%) and Europe (30%). One notable regional difference was that external advisers were counted among key decision makers more often in Europe (17%) than in Asia-Pacific (5%) and the United States (2%).
30 Rockefeller Philanthropy Advisors (n 2).
31 For more on specific methods of assessment, see Rockefeller Philanthropy, *Assessing Impact*, www.rockpa.org/wp-content/uploads/2017/08/Assessing-Impact.pdf.

# III. Decision making in family philanthropy

**Etienne Eichenberger**
WISE – philanthropy advisors, Switzerland
**Małgorzata Kurak**
**Peter Vogel**
IMD Business School

### 1. Introduction

Family businesses around the world contribute significantly to the economic and societal wellbeing of many nations.[1] The vast majority of enterprising families are active in philanthropy, either personally or through their companies.[2] In philanthropy, enterprising families can provide relief, or even solutions, where no one else (eg, governments, profit-oriented entities or global communities) would dare to intervene.[3] However, philanthropy is not just important from a societal and environmental standpoint.[4] Philanthropy can also play a significant role for the families themselves.[5] Philanthropy can become a catalyst for the transmission of values and beliefs; it can serve as a platform for education of family members (in particular, next-generation members); and it can act as the glue between family members or branches, across generations.[6]

However, giving is complex – and it can become even more complex when one is giving together with other family members.[7] One crucial – and challenging for many families – element of philanthropy is decision making. Family philanthropists need to make important decisions constantly.[8] There are many diverse decisions that need to be taken, including the focus in giving (eg, children, education, health); the geography you are focusing on (eg, locally, nationally, globally); the degree of involvement of different family members; the partnerships you need to build to successfully navigate your philanthropic journey; the types and amount of resources you wish to devote; and the most appropriate governance structure for your giving.

Based on an in-depth research project in which we interviewed over 70 philanthropically active families, and on our decades of experience working with philanthropic families, we identified at least 32 trade-offs that must be decided on at some point during the philanthropic journey. Clearly, some questions are more relevant than others to get started and the questions will largely depend on your philanthropic purpose, goals and ambitions. We start this chapter by providing you with key guiding questions[9] that both novice and seasoned philanthropists need to consider in order to structure their decision-making processes:

- Which decisions would you like to take as a family and which governing body should be taking them (eg, family council, philanthropy committee, next-generation council, foundation board, foundation management, family office)?
- How will you be taking decisions as a family (eg, on projects, financial matters, strategic matters)?
- Which decisions do you delegate to other governance bodies within your family enterprise system (eg, family office, company board of directors)?
- How formal do you want your philanthropy governance to be?
- How can you progress while learning to improve your approach? Will your decision-making processes be linked to your data reports or benchmarks?

To provide guidance in navigating these important questions, we present the types of decisions that enterprising families need to make on their philanthropic journey. We then provide insights on how philanthropic decision making can become a more integrated aspect of the family enterprise system. Finally, we share learnings and recommendations collected through years of experience working with and researching successful family philanthropists.

## 2. What do enterprising families say about decision making in philanthropy?

Family philanthropy is a journey that often starts with an individual and, over time, can turn into a collective family journey, which raises several challenges when it comes to decision making. Even though families may perceive their philanthropy as a collective effort, decision making often does not reflect this collective nature; and while certain formal structures may be in place, the actual process of decision making may happen more informally. In the following, we will share five selected and illustrative statements that were made by interviewees.

Often, the founder, patriarch or matriarch makes the most critical decisions, even long after the younger generations have taken over various responsibilities of the family's philanthropic work, as illustrated by the following statement:

> *We have this committee and councils, but this is only on paper, because the decisions are made outside of these councils and committees – by my father.*
> Interviewee 1, Gen 3, Switzerland

To avoid informal decision making, several families have put in place strict governance structures with clear policies and rules. This more formalised approach allows them to make decisions exclusively during dedicated meetings, and family members are instructed not to discuss any relevant topics outside of these meetings, as illustrated in this statement by one interviewee:

> *We are pretty independent in the sense that our [foundation's] management is independent and our [foundation's] board is independent, so the family members don't really get involved in terms of what to do or how to do it; we [at the foundation] do that on our own. But we do make it a practice to report back to the rest of the family.*
> Interviewee 2, Gen 4, Singapore

At the other end of the spectrum, we have observed some families which have very informal structures with basically no policies or procedures in place to regulate decision making. As a result, their decisions are made on an *ad hoc* basis, as reflected in the following statement:

> *All of our family members (including spouses) are equal partners in decision making.*
>
> *There are no formal policies or documents to regulate our giving. The approach is that family comes first, and our decision making is very value driven.*
> Interviewee 3, Gen 3, Luxembourg

Either way, decision making dominated by one individual or a group of individuals (eg, founder(s), senior generation, family leader(s)) can become a source of tension between the family members, or even entire generations, as can be seen in the following example:

> *Our frustration is that we were never asked the question of how we wanted to handle philanthropy in our generation; we were basically confronted with the decision of the senior generation saying: "You*

*will handle philanthropy like this, and that's it." That's the frustration we had, and it's created a few disagreements.*
Interviewee 4, Gen 3, Switzerland

If family members do not enjoy a sufficient level of autonomy in the giving process, there can be a danger of mission drift and disengagement of the rest of the family from their philanthropy. Further disadvantages can lead to a lack of opportunity for family members to explore and develop their own giving profile, learn how to 'stand on their own two feet' and take a leadership role in philanthropy. Ideally, decision making in philanthropy would be designed to enable inclusive, transparent and fair decisions. The following example nicely illustrates such a giving model:

*We have a foundation board ... and we also have an assembly of donors – we gather twice a year – and we have voting rights. All the decisions are being made in the board, and then they are validated during the assembly of donors. Because we wanted to empower younger donors, who, on average, give less money than more senior donors, we have developed a decision-making system in which one donor receives one vote, and we also give an additional vote per tranche of €50,000 donated.*
Interviewee 5, Gen 5, Belgium

**3. Heterogeneity of decisions in family philanthropy**

One important purpose of family philanthropy, beyond the cause itself, is to include the family in a joint project. Family philanthropists need to consider how they can achieve that in practice and encourage clear and structured involvement of their families. The way in which founders include the nuclear as well as the wider family in philanthropic decision making will shape their involvement for generations to come.

Families are faced with several decisions – so-called 'trade-offs' – related to family philanthropy. As we discovered through our research, philanthropic trade-offs require a careful reflection and in-depth discussions among family members. Trade-offs are presented as a spectrum, with two opposing views and many hybrid solutions in between. Different family members likely have a range of views with respect to where they would like to position their family's philanthropic efforts. A clear decision-making process is crucial to navigate these various trade-offs effectively and ultimately to help enterprising families to achieve their desired philanthropic impact.

Although important to boost family involvement in philanthropy, the list of trade-offs is not exhaustive. The 32 trade-offs we uncovered represent the critical decisions with respect to a family's philanthropic journey – related to the *why*, *what*, *who* and *how* of their giving. In this section, we introduce four trade-offs related to family involvement in order to illustrate the importance of good decision-making processes and structures as part of a family's philanthropic journey.

**Trade-off 1: Individual versus nuclear family versus wider family**

**Figure 1. Individual versus nuclear family versus wider family**

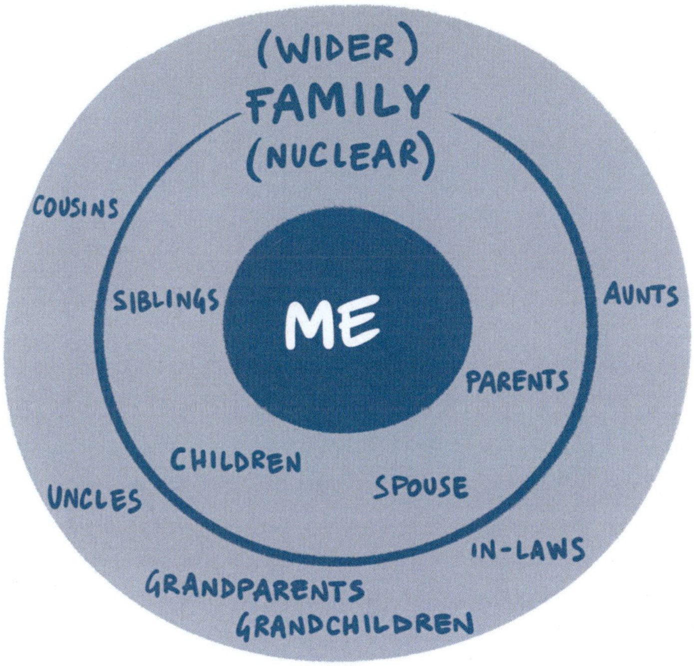


*Source: Adapted from Vogel* et al, *2020.*

Families differ in size, complexity and dynamics; and it follows that there are many ways to involve family members in philanthropy. Deciding which family members to involve – and in what manner – begins with a reflection of what your own role will be, before considering whether members of your immediate family can and should be involved, followed by your wider family. This process can be complicated, requiring careful diplomacy, clarity and foresight. These are some illustrative questions you need to ask yourself in order to come to a decision on this trade-off:

- Do you want to give on your own?
- Do you want to include your nuclear family only or spread the net wider?
- Are there specific branches of the family that you want to engage with?
- Do you want to combine the resources of a range of members from across the wider family with varying levels of responsibility and in different roles?
- Will you include in-laws or children from later marriages?

#### Trade-off 2: Single generation versus multiple generations

| Single generation | ⟷ | Multiple generations |
|---|---|---|
| Engage only one generation in your giving | | Engage two or more generations in your giving |

Family philanthropy can focus primarily on the close-knit activity of siblings or it can extend to include engagement across several generations – perhaps as a way to build unity, onboard the next generation or transfer values. Each approach – and every iteration in between – has its strengths and weaknesses, and also ties back to the purpose of your giving. For example, engaging several generations can require an awareness of the diverse tensions and perspectives that exist between older and younger members of your family.

- Are you interested in working only with your siblings or cousins, perhaps to build bonds or pursue common interests?
- Do you want to empower the next generation, pass on certain values or embrace philanthropy as a way to onboard younger relatives into the family enterprise system?
- Has there been a change of family leadership or circumstances that requires a rethink of who is involved?
- Do you have new ambitions for a close-knit project to involve younger generations?

#### Trade-off 3: Hands-on versus hands-off

| Hands-on | ⟷ | Hands-off |
|---|---|---|
| Being closely involved in leading your philanthropic activities | | Delegate operational activities in your giving to others |

For each family member, it is important to clarify the exact nature of philanthropic involvement. At one end of the spectrum, the entire adventure may be operationally 'hands-off', where you and your family set the focus and ambitions for your giving, but then outsource the rest to external partners or hire professional employers. At the other end of the spectrum, the family might want to be intensely involved in the management of every step of the process and get truly 'hands-on' on the ground. There is clearly a myriad of options in between – and the best balance will depend on the specific expectations and needs of your family. Many enterprising families balance their involvement between the two, engaging where they can while hiring advisers to guide them and partners to implement their giving in concrete projects.

- How hands-on or hands-off do you want to – or can you – and your family be in your giving?
- Do you want to select a handful of family members for key, 'hands-on' roles, while asking others to take more of a back seat?
- Do your family members want to be involved?
- What level of engagement do you expect from your family members?
- What roles do your family members want to play?

**Trade-off 4: Bloodline first versus competency first**

| Bloodline first | ←——→ | Competency first |
|---|---|---|
| Access and right to involvement are based on being a (bloodline) descendent of the founder | | Access and right to involvement are based on qualifications, achievements and capabilities |

If you wish your philanthropy to be both family controlled and family run, the question of legitimacy, access and responsibilities might grow as the family grows. This could mean either only allowing bloodline relatives to be part of your philanthropic journey or allowing involvement purely on professional qualifications and expertise; or it could just as well mean a mixed approach. As you don't – legally speaking – own a foundation that serves the public interest, it might be helpful and relevant to reflect on the core principles that you want to adopt regarding your family's involvement, and especially the spouses. Principles can change, but it is important to continue to reflect over time on where the talent and the engagement come from.

- Will legitimacy, access or the right to be involved and make decisions depend on whether family members are direct descendants of the founders?
- Will you only base involvement decisions on professional skills and qualifications?
- If the family grows, how will the various competences and experiences of family members be harnessed and managed?
- Will you combine the two approaches in some way?

**4. Decision making in family philanthropy**
The majority of families' decision making is regulated in the bylaws – typically requiring a majority vote or unanimity. Each family should find the most appropriate decision-making process before venturing out and starting their philanthropic journey. The ultimate structure that philanthropists will choose for their giving will also depend on the other governance bodies within the family enterprise system.

Clearly, certain decisions are more important or strategic than others. As a result, you might want to consider which types of decisions might require the involvement of the family and which can be taken by other governance bodies (eg, the family office or employees in the foundation). If you don't clearly spell out how decisions will be made, you might end up having conflicts within the family that could have easily been avoided had the rules of the game been defined upfront.

However, as with every decision that is taken inside a family, these can be incredibly time-consuming and frustrating processes. Even if you have an explicit approach towards decision making, other family dynamics can kick in and bypass the formal governance you have created. A typical challenge arises when one board member (eg, the founder or senior family member) has more influence than others and,

**Figure 2. Family philanthropy as an important element of the family enterprise system**

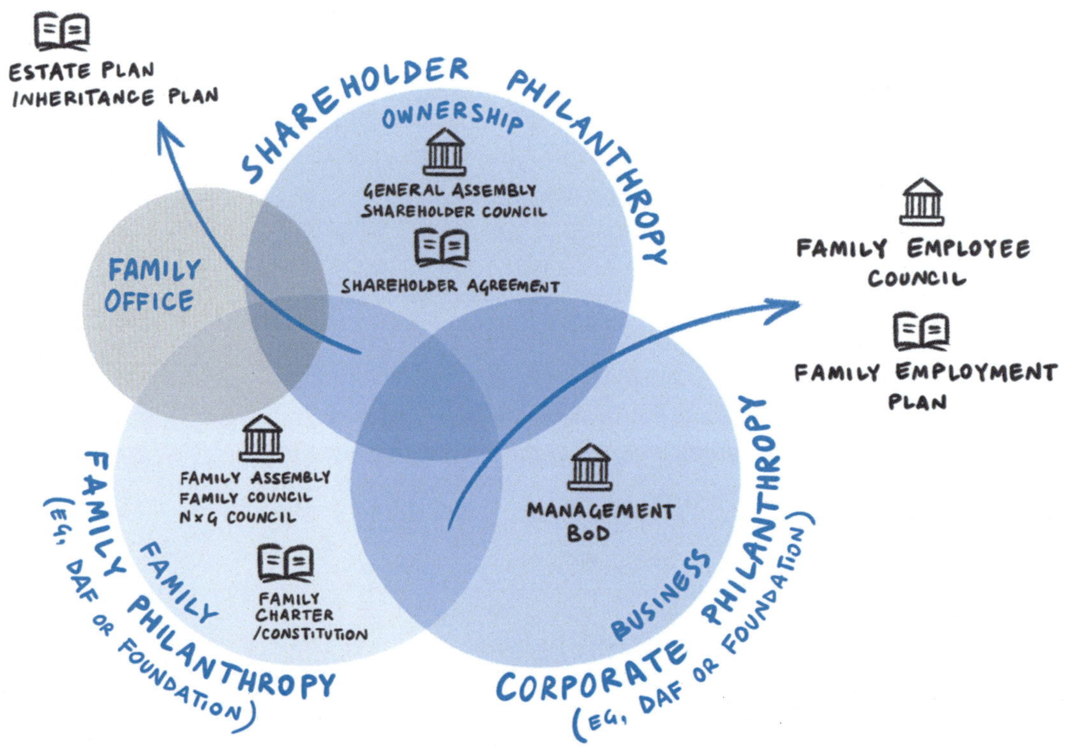


*Source: Adapted from Vogel* et al, *2020.*

*"It is of critical importance that you clearly spell out who, or which governing body, will take what types of decisions and based on what types of decision-making mechanism. Aligning this with your overall governance will help you to establish a more effective and efficient philanthropic endeavour."*

consequently, their opinion implicitly carries more weight than that of the others. This can be particularly frustrating for the next generation, for outside advisers or for independent foundation board members who have been hired to help professionalise giving. It is therefore important that all family members understand and, as much as possible, follow the governance that the family has agreed on. It is of critical importance that you clearly spell out who, or which governing body, will take what types of decisions and based on what types of decision-making mechanism. Aligning this with your overall governance will help you to establish a more effective and efficient philanthropic endeavour.

In Table 1 we share the three most common approaches for decision making in family philanthropy.

**Table 1. Common approaches for decision making in family philanthropy**

| | |
|---|---|
| **Unilateral decision making** | • This is a quick and efficient mechanism that is useful for trivial or uncontroversial decisions or decisions that need to be made in a very short timeframe (eg, disaster or emergency grant making).<br>• This type of decision making may be found in the early phase of a philanthropic engagement, before formal governance structures are in place.<br>• In enterprising families, we may be confronted with unilateral decision making (eg, because there is one dominant family member). |
| **Board voting with majority** | • This approach might be required by the bylaws for a certain type of decision. The process involves all board members and leads to a definite outcome based on whether a majority is reached.<br>• Board voting with majority can also be a useful mechanism where philanthropy spans and involves different parts of the family enterprise system, such as the family, the business, the ownership group and the family office.<br>• Voting is often considered as a fallback option if consensus cannot be reached. |
| **Consensus-based decision making** | • Consensus-based decision making may be required by the bylaws for very important decisions (eg, discontinuing the foundation). It is a mechanism that typically involves a lot of discussions that ultimately lead to consensus, thus producing a shared understanding and buy-in.<br>• Consensus-based decision making can also be a sign of a very healthy and functioning family, ownership group or business board. We know from best practice corporate boards that they decide based on consensus quite naturally and only in rare instances must revert to voting by majority.<br>• However, in case of different views and perspectives – which are inevitable in a family and even more so if multiple stakeholders from the family enterprise system are involved – this can be a very time-consuming process. The attempt to reach consensus might trigger other forms of conflicts (depending on the family dynamics), which is why it might not be the most appropriate form of decision making for every family and every decision. |

**5. De-risking philanthropic decisions**

Professional philanthropists are carefully considering whether their giving – which evidently is designed to have a positive impact on a specific stakeholder group – might have a negative impact that was not previously considered. Therefore, to de-risk their philanthropic investments, they start integrating due diligence and follow-up processes to monitor how their philanthropic resources are utilised and what their overall impact is. In general, the families that we work with suggest that they feel a great responsibility to ensure that their financial and non-financial resources are used in the most effective and efficient way. To build a sound decision-making process, it is recommended that family philanthropists stay informed and rigorous; make timely decisions; and actively assess risks. Every philanthropic decision carries certain risks that need to be considered. These risks might include:

- compliance with law and regulations;
- giving to political (or arguable) causes; and
- collateral damage and reputation.

However, not all risks affect one's giving in the same way. While it is impossible to rule out any potential negative impact of one's actions, it is important to assess and prioritise philanthropic risks. It is recommended to consider the following aspects:

- Degree of severity: The quality or state of a failure being severe or very bad;
- Probability of occurrence: The likelihood that a particular failure will occur; and
- Ability to prevent: The possibility to keep a failure from happening.

**6. Learnings and recommendations**

Any organisation has its own lifecycle, from creation to termination. This is no different for philanthropy. Across this cycle, families must manage the operational challenges of establishing or running a philanthropic organisation, such as asset control, start-up costs, management and administrative costs and taxes.[10] Beyond this, there are other challenges to be met and overcome – for example, a diminishing family interest in a cause due to dispersed multi-generational interests or maybe, over time, the focus of your giving becoming less important.

Being prepared to renew any philanthropic organisation while instilling a spirit of continuous learning and improvement will help to ensure that your giving remains relevant and effective. Our experience shows that motivations often remain consistent over generations, but priorities can change.

Here, we provide some examples of ways in which enterprising families navigate the decision making in their philanthropy:

- 'Taking the pulse' of the family is a useful way to avoid uncomfortable voting situations or to determine how close the family is to reaching consensus.
- Before presenting a proposal during an annual family gathering or regular board meeting, test the ground and prepare the family. It might seem like a time-consuming process, but you are more likely to get the support you are looking for.
- Integrate voting rights in the philanthropic decision-making process to balance out the fact that the senior generation donates, on average, more money than the younger generation.
- Put the beneficiaries at the centre of decision making. An awareness of local culture is crucial in making the best decisions in one's giving (even if they might not seem 'odd' at the time).
- Delegate when appropriate. Hear the voice of your family and partners, and delegate when appropriate. To achieve greater impact, you will need to delegate decision-making power and acknowledge your own limitations.
- Openly and explicitly discuss issues in philanthropy, as this strengthens the family's morale and sense of togetherness.
- Before making important decisions, agree on a fallback decision-making method, as this can prevent families from being stuck in a disagreement for an extended period of time.

### 7. Conclusion

Effective decision making in philanthropy is an important pillar in achieving greater impact through giving. It helps to create a more neutral ground to approach decisions within the family which, over time, will inevitably become a more integrated element of the family enterprise system. Good decision making is necessary for the management of giving, the involvement of the family and governance coordination across the entire system. Joined experience in philanthropy helps to create a shared legacy that giving is part and parcel of life, which ultimately helps family members to become better humans and better decision makers.

*"Effective decision making in philanthropy is an important pillar in achieving greater impact through giving. It helps to create a more neutral ground to approach decisions within the family which, over time, will inevitably become a more integrated element of the family enterprise system."*

## Notes

1 *Tharawat Magazine* (2014) "What is the Economic Impact of Family Businesses?", www.tharawat-magazine.com/economic-impact-family-businesses.
2 N Feliu and IC Botero (2016) "Philanthropy in Family Enterprises: A Review of Literature", *Family Business Review*, 29(1), 121–141, https://doi.org/10.1177/0894486515610962; RA Litz and AC Stewart (2000) "Charity begins at home: Family firms and patterns of community involvement", *Nonprofit and Voluntary Sector Quarterly*, 29(1), 131–148, https://doi.org/10.1177/0899764000291008.
3 National Philanthropic Trust (2021) "Charitable Giving Statistics", www.nptrust.org/philanthropic-resources/charitable-giving-statistics/.
4 A Gautier and AC Pache (2015) "Research on Corporate Philanthropy: A Review and Assessment", *Journal of Business Ethics*, 126(3), 343–369, https://doi.org/10.1007/s10551-013-1969-7; TMN Schuyt (2010) "Philanthropy in European welfare states: A challenging promise?", *International Review of Administrative Sciences*, 76(4), 774–789, https://doi.org/10.1177/0020852310381218.
5 P Vogel, E Eichenberger and M Kurak (2020) *The Family Philanthropy Navigator: The Inspirational Guide for Philanthropic Families on Their Giving Journey* (IMD Publishing).
6 P Vogel (2018) "Trends in Family Philanthropy", www.imd.org/research-knowledge/articles/trends-in-family-philanthropy.
7 B Breeze (2009) "Natural philanthropists: Findings of the family business philanthropy and social responsibility inquiry", www4.dcu.ie/sites/default/files/centre_for_family_ business/natural-philanthropists.pdf; G Campopiano, A de Massis and F Chirico (2014) "Firm Philanthropy in Small- and Medium-Sized Family Firms: The Effects of Family Involvement in Ownership and Management", *Family Business Review*, 27(3), 244–258, https://doi.org/10.1177/0894486514538450.
8 Vogel, Eichenberger and Kurak (n 5).
9 *Ibid.*
10 D Brody and C Strauch (1990) "Who Are the Family Foundations' Findings from the Foundation *Management Survey", Family Business Review*, 3(4), 337–346, https://doi.org/10.1111/j.1741-6248.1990.00337.x.

# IV. Methods and legal structure of giving

**Peter Cafferkey**
EVPA
**James Maloney**
Farrer & Co

Families approaching philanthropy for the first time – and even those who have some experience in philanthropic giving and, perhaps because of a major life event, are looking afresh at the approach they take – may find the array of choices increasingly overwhelming.

There is often an initial decision concerning the jurisdiction of any giving structure. There may be a choice as to whether to set up a separate giving structure or give through an existing legal vehicle. If a separate structure is preferred, there may be further choices concerning the type of structure to use and, importantly, whether to seek tax-exempt or charitable status in the jurisdiction in question. Finally, of course, there are important questions about the family's approach to philanthropy, what they want it to achieve and what impact they want it to have.

In this chapter, we aim to demystify some of the most significant questions that philanthropically minded families face – while also acknowledging that the approach a family takes to philanthropy will be shaped by choices they make, both at the start and as their experience deepens their knowledge (and as their circumstances evolve); and that no family can be expected to know everything at the outset.

**1. Choice of jurisdiction**

In an era of increasing globalisation, families wish to understand the options available to them, including the legal structures available, and increasingly are making comparisons and choices between jurisdictions.

This choice is guided by a number of important considerations, including:

- whether a jurisdiction offers the philanthropic family the possibility of tax relief on donations they may make;
- the degree of flexibility that a jurisdiction affords in relation to the scope of projects that the philanthropic family might wish to fund, in terms of both their nature and location;
- whether and to what extent a jurisdiction's regulation of philanthropic structures imposes restrictions on the nationality and residence of those exercising decision-making control and how that might affect the family;
- the extent of regulation in a jurisdiction and the administrative requirements that this regulation places on philanthropists; and
- the reputation of a jurisdiction and its regulator, particularly if funds are to be sought from other parties as well as donated by the family.

**2. Tax relief**

For many philanthropic families, tax relief is a significant consideration. While philanthropists are generally not motivated solely or even mainly by tax benefits, there is understandably a widespread wish among most donors to give as tax efficiently as possible.

Here it is important to consider the nature of the gift. Philanthropists may donate in the form of cash gifts or through non-monetary or 'in-kind' donations. Forms of non-monetary donation may include:

- gifts of property;
- gifts of stocks and shares;
- gifts of art and other cultural assets;
- gifts of other personal property; and
- gifts in the form of the donor's time through volunteering.

The extent to which each of these forms of gift is recognised in the tax system varies considerably from jurisdiction to jurisdiction.

The United States has a long-established and well-developed tradition of charitable giving, and its tax system has developed to reflect this through the deductibility of donations. Conversely, the United Kingdom and Ireland operate a matching scheme, where governments

*"Some philanthropic families will want to understand the scope for cross-border philanthropy to be recognised for tax purposes. For the most part, tax deductions are available for those with local-source income who donate to entities in the jurisdiction."*

top up donations at a given rate so that the entity receiving the donation can claim the tax relief (and, depending on the rate of tax they pay, donors may also receive relief).

Some degree of recognition of charitable giving is a feature of many tax codes, although reliefs work in different ways in different jurisdictions (with both the scale of and eligibility for reliefs varying widely). This variation was observed in a 2020 Organisation for Economic Co-operation and Development (OECD) report on taxation and philanthropy. In some countries surveyed, donations are deductible; other countries offer tax credits; and in some cases, donations are matched or facilitated through an allocation scheme.[1]

Some philanthropic families will want to understand the scope for cross-border philanthropy to be recognised for tax purposes. For the most part, tax deductions are available for those with local-source income who donate to entities in the jurisdiction. The availability of reliefs for non-nationals or for those who do not pay tax in the relevant jurisdiction, or where the donation is to an overseas entity, is more fragmentary.

As the OECD's 2020 report on taxation and philanthropy noted: "despite fairly widespread use of incentives for domestic philanthropy, the landscape for a more global approach to philanthropy remains fairly guarded ... the general position is that the relief available for donations to domestic philanthropic entities is not available for donations to foreign entities."[2]

There are limited situations where tax relief may be available for donations to foreign entities:

- in member states of the European Union and the European Economic Area that are subject to rulings of the Court of Justice of the European Union (CJEU);
- in some nations that have bilateral agreements that permit cross-border tax relief (eg, the US-Canada and US-Mexico tax treaties); and
- in some nations (eg, Canada and New Zealand) that have a process for recognising foreign charitable entities in limited circumstances and allowing tax relief for donations to those entities.

The position in many European jurisdictions changed following the CJEU judgments in three important cases which established that applying charitable tax reliefs only to organisations established in a donor's member state was contrary to the European Union's non-discrimination principle and, as such, a breach of the free movement of capital. Accordingly, charitable gifts by EU donors to non-domestic charities should be entitled to the same tax reliefs as gifts made to domestic charities.[3] (The same is also true for the reliefs applicable to the recipient organisation[4] and in relation to the effect of charitable reliefs on inheritance tax.)[5]

The welcome outcome of these judgments is confirmation that philanthropic giving is protected by the European Union's fundamental freedoms; although unfortunately, implementation has been incomplete. Even where the letter of the judgments has been implemented, the spirit of the law has been hampered by comparability tests.[6] Such tests continue to complicate the position for donors and charitable organisations seeking to benefit from cross-border tax reliefs.

Other than in the exceptional cases mentioned above, recognition of cross-border giving remains limited. This creates difficulty for philanthropists seeking to claim tax relief where the donor is a non-national or does not pay tax in the relevant jurisdiction, or where the donation is to an overseas entity.

One frequent solution for a charitable entity seeking the support of donors wishing to obtain tax relief in another jurisdiction is to establish a supporters' or 'friends of' charity in the donor's home jurisdiction. Many jurisdictions allow such an entity to be established to support the overseas recipient charity, provided that its purposes are charitable under the law of the home jurisdiction.

**3. Other jurisdictional considerations**

Philanthropic families considering where to establish a giving structure are unlikely to be guided solely by the availability of tax reliefs, even where this may be an important issue. Many families wish to understand the degree of flexibility that a jurisdiction affords in terms of how the funds can be applied and the extent of regulation in that jurisdiction.

This latter point can cut both ways, of course. If a family wishes to raise funds from or collaborate with other parties, or is concerned about how funds may be handled by future generations, they may prefer to establish the structure in a jurisdiction such as the United States or the United Kingdom, where there is a well-developed legal framework for charities and registration with the relevant regulator (eg, the Internal Revenue Service in the United States; or specific charity regulatory bodies such as the regulators that exist in England and Wales, Scotland and Northern Ireland).

*"Philanthropic families considering where to establish a giving structure are unlikely to be guided solely by the availability of tax reliefs, even where this may be an important issue."*

If, on the other hand, the entity being established is unlikely to raise funds from or enter into contracts with third parties, and the family wishes to prioritise flexibility, the administrative burden and regulatory scrutiny involved in establishing a structure in a highly regulated jurisdiction such as the United States or the United Kingdom may prove less attractive. In this situation, a family's priority may be to minimise regulation and to preserve their anonymity; and in this case offshore jurisdictions (eg, Jersey or Guernsey) may be preferable.

Practical considerations include:

- any nationality or residency requirements for those managing a giving structure, including whether there is a requirement for a local fiduciary; and
- whether there are requirements to hold meetings in the jurisdiction.

While these factors may rarely seem as important as tax and other funding considerations, they will have implications for identifying who can manage the philanthropic venture.

*"One pervasive consideration in any jurisdiction is whether a particular legal structure affords a separate legal personality and, for those running the structure, the benefit of limited liability."*

**4. Structures and organisations**

There is an important initial question about whether a separate structure is needed. Setting up a new entity is not always the right approach for a philanthropically minded family. Significant commitments are involved in running a separate entity and some philanthropists therefore prefer to use a donor-advised fund (DAF). This is an existing charitable vehicle that allows donors to give tax effectively and to recommend donations from their contributions. DAFs are explored further in Chapter VII.

If a separate structure is preferred, however, different jurisdictions offer a varying range of legal structures for charitable giving.

Many civil law jurisdictions (eg, Switzerland and Liechtenstein, among others in Western Europe) use a variant of the term 'foundation' to describe a distinct legal entity that can be used by families for philanthropic giving. In other countries, however, organisations through which philanthropic families give can be structured in different ways, using a range of legal vehicles, and the term 'foundation' may have no specific meaning. In the United Kingdom, for example, it is possible for a philanthropic entity to be established as a company, a trust, an unincorporated association, a charitable incorporated organisation or another type of entity – and in any of these cases, to be called a 'foundation'.

The structures available and the legal considerations applicable to each will vary from jurisdiction to jurisdiction. One pervasive consideration in any jurisdiction is whether a particular legal structure affords a separate legal personality and, for those running the structure, the benefit of limited liability. With legal structures that do offer this, it is the entity in its corporate name, rather than the individuals running it, which enters into contracts, holds assets and may sue and be sued.

Conversely, unincorporated structures have no legal personality of their own. It is the individuals running the organisation, rather than the organisation itself, who enter into contracts; execute documents; hold the assets of the organisation; and can sue and be sued. Those individuals may be personally jointly and severally liable for the debts and liabilities of the organisations – an important consideration.

In some jurisdictions, it is usual for the vehicles through which philanthropic families support good causes to do little more than make grants, which may (depending on the law of that jurisdiction) restrict the liability to which philanthropists are exposed.

This is not always the case. In the United Kingdom, for example, if an organisation is to employ staff, own or manage land, or carry out any activities of its own beyond simply making grants (or if it is possible that it may wish to do any of these things in the future), it is generally more appropriate for it to be established as an incorporated structure. This has led to the increasing popularity of structures such as the company limited by guarantee and the charitable incorporated organisation in the United Kingdom.

In many jurisdictions, eligibility for the entity itself to benefit from tax reliefs and for its donors to be able to make tax-efficient donations depends on charitable status and/or recognition as a tax-exempt body. This may involve a registration process (which in some jurisdictions may be complex), as well as ongoing reporting requirements.

For many common law jurisdictions, there are similarities in the kinds of purposes recognised as charitable which stem from a shared charity law lineage.[7] A donor should not assume, however, that simply because a given purpose is charitable in one jurisdiction, it will necessarily be considered charitable elsewhere. Even where jurisdictions are similar, there can be differences on points of detail (eg, those that exist between the constituent nations of the United Kingdom, where charity law is a devolved matter in Scotland and Northern Ireland).

**5. Trends for the future**

There have been a number of important trends in philanthropy in recent years.

One is an increasing interest in and tendency for philanthropists to use non-charitable structures. Four particular situations where this may be of interest are:

- where the family wishes to engage in supporting work that goes beyond what the law recognises as charitable;[8]
- where the family wishes to donate shares in a business they own to a giving structure they have set up, without coming up against complex rules concerning diversification (which could otherwise lead to the giving structure needing to consider selling those shares, depending on the legal requirements in the jurisdiction in question);
- where the family is concerned about greater transparency and more onerous reporting requirements; and
- where the family wishes to retain constitutional controls that may be difficult to reconcile with charity law requirements in the jurisdiction in question.[9]

English law does not permit the formation of non-charitable private purpose trusts other than in very limited circumstances; but in many jurisdictions (including the United Kingdom), there are options to use a corporate structure for a non-charitable, not-for-profit entity.

In some jurisdictions it may be possible for an organisation to carry out charitable activity while also allowing for the possibility of retaining funds for other, wider purposes (eg, by the donor family or by other non-charitable beneficiaries). Examples of 'hybrid' vehicles that can be used in this way are Jersey and Guernsey foundations, and Cayman Islands STAR trusts.

**6. Impact and the growth of venture philanthropy**

Philanthropists are also increasingly seeking to measure the impact of their donations through monitoring and reporting. Connected to this is the growth of so-called 'venture philanthropy', which allows philanthropists to use a range of ways of giving (including grants, loans and other forms of social investment) to support charitable organisations.

This is intrinsically connected to the question of what the family is looking for philanthropy to achieve.

This can include:

- the societal change they would like to see;
- how they would like that to happen; and
- importantly, the experience that they as a family want from this.

This is often the elephant in the room, with some families not wanting to be honest about this due to many factors. Some are limited by religion or beliefs, or a need to give back without any personal satisfaction or return. Others feel awkward discussing any benefit for themselves or family coming from the philanthropic arena. However, without addressing this element, it can often be difficult for families to bring their 'whole selves' to the philanthropy, confusing those charitable partners and over time breeding a lack of engagement or even resentment towards their philanthropy from other members of the family.

Venture philanthropy as one approach came about from this self-reflection. Individuals who realised that they enjoyed their commercial careers were proud of their skills and could not see why they should not bring those skills and experiences to their charitable endeavours. Alongside bringing more of themselves, they also saw the benefits that this transfer of skills could have for their charitable endeavours. Rather than just grant funds from a distance, they wanted to bring further non-financial support (examples such as providing mentoring or access to their networks), while also measuring and managing the impact in the way that they might have previously with other commercial investments.

From this, the three aspects of venture philanthropy were identified:

- the use of financial methods to suit the organisation (grants certainly, but also loans or other instruments if appropriate);
- relevant impact management and measurement (IMM); and
- the provision of non-financial support.

This full package of support enabled philanthropists to become far more involved in their giving, providing them with a sense of satisfaction that they were bringing their full selves to their giving and enabling them and their charity partners to achieve far more.

**Figure 1. Venture philanthropy roundel**

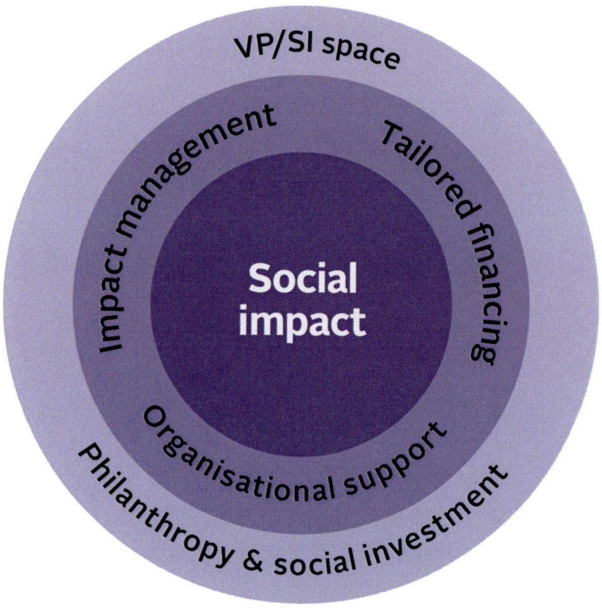


**Venture philanthropy (VP) is a high-engagement and long-term approach to generating social impact through three core practices:**

- **Tailored finance**
- **Organisational (non-financial) support**
- **Impact management**

However here, as with any successful philanthropic approach, the key factor was putting the societal problem at the centre of approaches and/or supporting the needs of those organisations looking to solve these societal challenges. By marrying more closely the needs of those with the knowledge and experience to the ambition of the donor, this approach can become a win-win to drive greater success and long-term engagement for both parties.

To start this process, families need to look at the role they wish to play both now and in the future. This leads to questions such as:

- whether they wish to be a capital provider (providing support to other delivery organisations) or whether they wish to be the practical delivery arm;
- the level of time and engagement that they and other family members wish to play on an ongoing basis; and

- how they see this playing a role with wider objectives such as family unity, dynamics and long-term wealth planning.

These questions have no 'right or wrong' answers; neither are they questions for which the answers will remain the same over time.

That said, families looking to make decisions on their philanthropic engagement need to consider these aspects. Here the use of external expertise and advice can be particularly beneficial, asking those questions, helping families to navigate their thinking, sharing examples and introducing families to peers who may have also gone through this process and can share learning. Existing regional networks, such as the European Venture Philanthropy Association[10] (EVPA) and Synergos' Global Philanthropist Circle,[11] married to national philanthropy collectives such as the recently launched Beacon Collaborative[12] in the United Kingdom, provide increasing opportunities for peer learning in a safe and supportive space for experiences to be shared among philanthropists.

The remaining key choice that drives structuring decisions is to identify the problem that, as a family, they wish to solve. This is a daunting but valuable exercise. Again, the input of peers or sharing of examples can be very helpful; as can the engagement of all members of the family. The outcome need not be exclusionary, as often families will look to have a number differing focus points. One large, often international, theme (eg, climate) can be married to smaller discretionary focuses led by children; or to enable support to local causes or even friends' fundraisers. This combined approach may require careful consideration at the time of creating a legal structure.

Some families have narrowed their focus based on geography (historic links, need or locations where they have a personal connection); others on age groups (young people, seniors); and still others by particular life experiences (healthcare due to personal loss and achievement due to family struggles are also common themes).

There is no right answer, and no family necessarily will or should be immediately able to answer this in a finite and everlasting manner. However, the key thing here is to be open, to learn and be prepared to refine this as more information is made available and family members grow in knowledge and experience. The adviser's role is crucial here in helping families to access information from outside of their normal networks. Subject experts can range from academics to those involved in policy to those with lived experience, all of whom can deepen the family's understanding; although the range of resources can be extensive and overwhelming. Family advisers can both help to synthesise this knowledge and provide a valuable service in protecting both family and charitable actors from unreasonable expectations, as an interface providing families with a degree of anonymity, while also removing the burden from subject experts and charitable organisations which are liable to overwork in the hope of substantial support.

Despite the challenges, research into an area will always help families to understand the situations and issues that they are looking to address through their philanthropy.

A constant wish to learn sits at the heart of all effective philanthropy and is the driver behind the IMM approach of venture philanthropy. Having identified the problem that they wish to address, families are moving on from the classic fiscal responsibility to show the use of funds, leading to a focus on the outcome (what changes) rather than the narrower outputs (what was done). As such, they are now looking to IMM as a tool to understand what is happening, not just to prove but always to improve – to increase the impact.

This desire to increase the level of family impact has also driven more families to look beyond the traditional model of philanthropic giving, where money is earned with one hand and given away with the other. Rather, they are exploring total impact, including both the way money is earned (through the rise of social responsible investment in the investment market and environmental, social and governance (ESG) criteria in the family business arena) and methods for philanthropic money itself to be recycled or to work harder.

Reflecting the primary driver behind decision making, families can look to invest either *for* or *with* impact.

For those investment decisions that are driven by asset creation or wealth protection over the long term, investment *with* impact can be incorporated to ensure that no harm is done (the basis for traditional ESG negative screening) or even to aim for a positive impact return while also not looking at any concession in financial return. This area of aiming for both impact and financial return, or 'impact investment', has been growing for over 10 years; and while still small (estimated at $715 billion globally in 2020 by the Global Impact Investing Network (GIIN)),[13] its wider impact can be seen in moves such as the pension with purpose movement in the United Kingdom[14] and disbursement campaigns against the fossil fuel industry.[15]

This investment-led portfolio can also be married to an active investing *for* impact portfolio, incorporating the family's philanthropy but also investments made where impact is non-negotiable and financial risk tolerance is higher.

**Figure 2. The impact ecosystem spectrum**

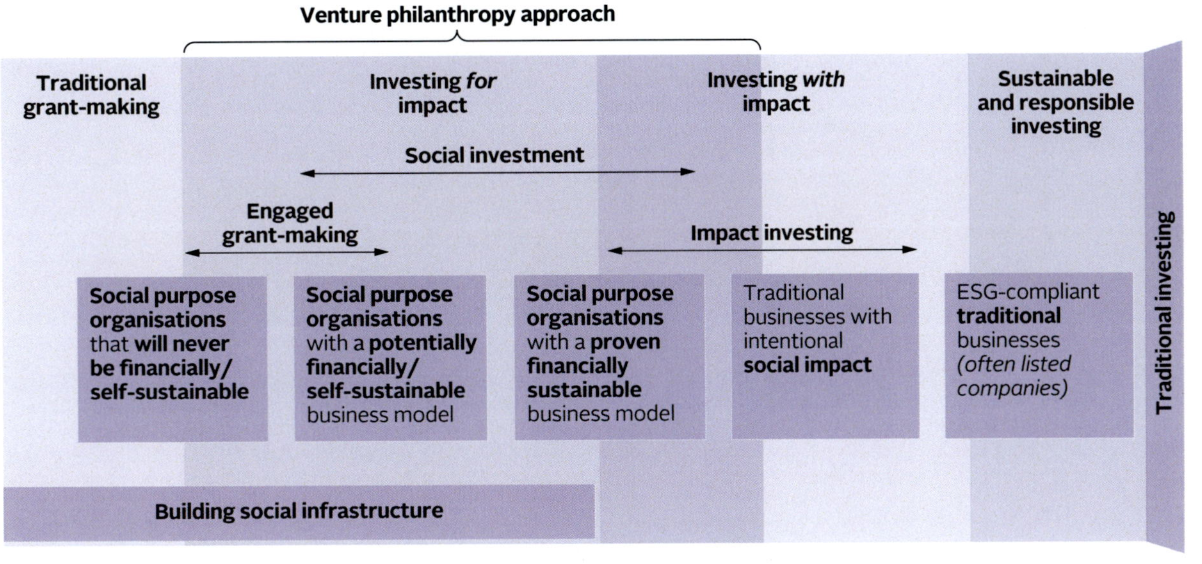


*Source: EVPA.*

Here it is important to clarify that this is not the case of one rather than the other; rather, they are complementary approaches. Depending on the needs of the organisations being supported and the ambitions of the philanthropist, a mix can be achieved.

In this way, families can increasingly point to an overall impact footprint across their investments. However, this puts more pressure on advisers looking to structure more flexibly and often increases the appeal of offshore over onshore structures, removing as it does some of the restrictions in charitable purpose and income generation.

This, like every other choice faced by family philanthropists, must be determined based on their own situation and ambitions. However, the key here is to learn by doing; learn by sharing; and learn by connecting through trusted advisers (whether traditional advisers such as law firms or those advising in slightly newer areas such as philanthropy advisers), existing not-for-profit networks (eg, EVPA, GIIN and Synergos) and leading academic institutions.

## 7. Conclusion

Philanthropy can be daunting, so all of us who work as advisers in this field should help families to remember that no one gets it right first time. Part of our role is to help them be open to learning through trial and error in a controlled way, providing the safety nets through effective structuring to allow families to have an engaging, fulfilling and rewarding experience in philanthropy.

## Notes

1 OECD (2020) *Report on Taxation and Philanthropy*, www.oecd.org/ctp/taxation-and-philanthropy-df434a77-en.htm.
2 *Ibid.*
3 *Hein Persche v Finanzamt Lüdenscheid* (C-318/07).
4 *Centro di Musicologia Walter Stauffer v Finanzamt München für Körperschaften* (C-386/04).
5 *Missionswerk Werner Heukelbach eV v Belgian State* (C-25/10).
6 Such as the Finance Act 2010 conditions in the United Kingdom and equivalent legislation in other European jurisdictions.
7 In particular, from the preamble to the Charitable Uses Act of 1601 (also known as the Statute of Elizabeth).
8 Such as where there is a risk of falling foul of a prohibition on charitable organisations funding purposes that the law may regard as political.
9 Such as those explored in *Lehtimaki v Cooper* [2020] UKSC 33, concerning the Children's Investment Fund Foundation.
10 www.evpa.eu.com.
11 Global Philanthropists Circle hosted by Synergos: www.synergos.org/global-philanthropists-circle.
12 Beacon Collaborative in the United Kingdom: www.beaconcollaborative.org.uk.
13 Global Impact Investing Network; Dean Hand, Hannah Dithrich, Sophia Sunderji, Noshin Nova, *2020 Annual Impact Investor Survey*,
https://thegiin.org/research/publication/impinv-survey-2020.
14 Pensions for Purpose United Kingdom: www.pensionsforpurpose.com.
15 *The Guardian*; "World's biggest sovereign wealth fund to ditch fossil fuels" (June 2019), www.theguardian.com/business/2019/jun/12/worlds-biggest-sovereign-wealth-fund-to-ditch-fossil-fuels.

# V. Location of family charities: the Netherlands and beyond

**Ineke A Koele**
Koele Tax & Legal Perspecta

Charity regulations can differ significantly from country to country. Multinational families may consider a number of jurisdictions in deciding where to establish a charity. The Netherlands is one of the most liberal jurisdictions in this regard.

**1. Introduction**

When internationally active families are considering where to base their family charity, the flexibility of the legal framework is paramount. The concept of a charity for tax and legal purposes is always subject to requirements and restrictions which will determine the extent to which an extended family can pursue their philanthropic vision.

In order to create a meaningful structure and take advantage of the legal framework in the optimal jurisdiction for a family's charitable activities, time and effort must be devoted to creating a meaningful nexus with that jurisdiction. Residence and domicile should never be taken for granted, but should be considered carefully. The day-to-day management of the charity should normally be based in the jurisdiction of choice.

If the family is resident elsewhere, or in several countries around the globe, the charity may also take on the function of a family council gathering, by involving representatives of the family in its governance.

The ideal legal framework should allow the family to participate in the governance of a charity, even if they do not have a nexus with the particular jurisdiction in which the charity is established.

The tax deductibility of the transfer of an endowed fund into a family charity is a decisive factor in only a few scenarios. If the family is resident in the Netherlands, the transfer to a foreign-based qualifying charitable entity can benefit from a tax deduction; but that is not the case everywhere in the world. In most jurisdictions, direct or indirect impediments prevent international grants from benefiting from tax deductions on the same basis as transfers to a local charity.[1] However, within the EU legal framework, the principle of non-discrimination should lead to full deductibility.

When examining the legal landscape for charities around the world, a good starting point is the research conducted by the US-based Hudson Institute, referred to as the "Index of Philanthropic Freedom".[2]

The United States and the United Kingdom are well known for their sophisticated but highly regulated legal and tax framework for charities; but the Netherlands is widely regarded as the most liberal jurisdiction in the world for philanthropic organisations, according to the Hudson Institute.

*"The United States and the United Kingdom are well known for their sophisticated but highly regulated legal and tax framework for charities; but the Netherlands is widely regarded as the most liberal jurisdiction in the world for philanthropic organisations, according to the Hudson Institute."*

Foundations – the most common legal form for charities in the Netherlands – have historically been part of the 'private domain' rather than the 'public domain', which means that there is limited regulatory oversight. Only in a catastrophic situation and at the request of a close circle of 'interested persons' will the local court and prosecutor have supervisory powers.

This is not the case in other continental European jurisdictions. For example, foundations in Switzerland, Germany and Denmark are closely scrutinised by local regulators. In the Netherlands, the concept of a 'charity' is relevant only for tax purposes; and a foundation that does not have the tax status of a charity (ANBI) may also pursue philanthropic causes. The traditional but sophisticated charity regimes in the United Kingdom and the United States provide for detailed regulatory oversight of family charities.[3] This is not only very expensive, but also unnecessarily restrictive.

There is a cultural resistance to greater regulation of foundations in the Netherlands. Non-profit organisations tend to complain about the administrative burden that they would have to bear if they were obliged to publish accounts, which currently is not compulsory for foundations in general. The Netherlands is also the first country in the world to have completely opened its borders to facilitate tax-efficient cross-border gifts and bequests (if the foreign charity has sought recognition as a charity under Dutch tax laws).

While the scope of regulatory oversight and restrictions for charities is important to consider when determining the optimal location of a family charity, there are also other factors to bear in mind in this respect.

First, the possibility of exiting from the jurisdiction should always be considered. If adverse (tax) legislation would affect the family charity, a mechanism should be put in place to withdraw funds and activities from the jurisdiction without stringent consequences.

Second, it should be considered whether the family charity in fact requires the status of a charity. Certain jurisdictions have a separate legal framework in place to govern charitable organisations, independently from the tax authorities which are responsible for ensuring that charities are tax compliant. In many situations, a charity must have a specific tax status in order to benefit from effective taxation of the income realised from its investments. This leads to situations in which charities have a dual compliance obligation. In practice, it is increasingly apparent that the status of a charity is not in fact required. Under Dutch tax law, a foundation is exempt from tax on investment income regardless of its purposes. ANBI status is not required if the charity is, for example, an operational charity that organises its own philanthropic activities.

Third, when the tax status of a charity is required, because otherwise transfers of funds would be subject to high gift tax rates, it is important to consider how practical compliance will work in the jurisdiction of choice, and what time and costs will need to be allocated in this regard. These will vary depending on the level of compliance and bureaucracy.

This chapter outlines the features of Dutch charitable foundations and makes some practical comparisons between other jurisdictions and the Netherlands.

**2. Dutch charitable foundations**

Charities in the Netherlands are primarily structured as foundations and, to a lesser extent, as associations. This chapter focuses on the foundation.

A Dutch foundation is a legally autonomous ('corporate') form, with rights and obligations, but without any owners or persons with an interest therein. A foundation is created through a legal transaction before a notary. It has no members and its purpose is to realise the objects set out in its articles of association, with the aid of funds dedicated for this purpose (Book 2, Article 285(1) of the Civil Code).

A foundation is a 'purpose fund', which may serve purposes that do not necessarily relate to a class of designated beneficiaries.

Dutch law follows the 'incorporation principle', which means in effect that if a foundation is created according to Dutch law but is governed outside the Netherlands (ie, it is staffed by individuals who are resident outside the Netherlands and has no office or activities in the Netherlands), its internal order will still be governed by Dutch law. This is why many international non-governmental organisations choose to use Dutch foundations or associations as their supranational governance body, no matter where in the world they are staffed. If this supranational body is not effectively managed from the Netherlands, there is no tax residence in the Netherlands and the organisation generally need not qualify as a charity under Dutch tax law. However, a foreign-based charity can be recognised as a charity for the purpose of Dutch tax law – for example, to attract Dutch resident donors.

While, as a rule, a family foundation must have an office and an establishment somewhere, it is presumed that it will choose a central hub for its activities, which implies that it will be effectively managed in the place of its establishment. A clear position on the effective place

*"Regardless of whether a family charity is funding other organisations or is merely operational by nature, the governance of the charity is of paramount importance."*

of management will avoid disputes over this issue and the corresponding tax and regulatory implications. Regardless of whether a family charity is funding other organisations or is merely operational by nature, the governance of the charity is of paramount importance.

In the Netherlands, the tension between foreign resident family members and the effective local management is typically resolved through the use of a supervisory board with controlling powers. The family staffs the supervisory board, which has month-to-month or quarter-to-quarter controlling power. It also has the power to appoint and dismiss board members, and to approve certain important decisions. The supervisory board can also advise the board of directors on how to pursue the foundation's objective, without having the authority to act on behalf of the foundation.

In principle, the governance of a Dutch foundation can be as sophisticated as the family wishes. A foundation can have various bodies for different functions and may act as a vehicle for achieving the family's long-term values and goals, which are reflected by its philanthropic purposes.

Unlike the German-style foundations to be found in Germany, Austria and Switzerland, the Dutch foundation is not merely the embodiment of the wishes of the founder. The Dutch foundation is a constitutional entity; it can transform and adapt to changing circumstances. It is possible to include certain 'unamendable' provisions in the foundation's articles, whose amendment will require approval by the local court (although these are never strictly unamendable).

To recognise a charity for tax purposes, the following questions must be answered in the affirmative:

- Is the organisation a foundation, an association, a legal person under public law or a church institution?
- Does the organisation, according to both its organisational documents and its operational activities, operate on a non-profit basis?
- Is the organisation, according to both its organisational documents and its operational activities, pursuing a public interest (nearly) exclusively?
- Is it ensured that members of the board of directors or other third parties cannot dispose of the assets of the organisation as if they were their own?
- Do the members of the board of directors, both factually and according to the regulations, conduct their activities without remuneration (except for attendance fees and/or expense allowances)?

*"A family should always consider what the default position would be in a jurisdiction. In fact, this should be the first question they consider."*

- Does the organisation have a policy plan which provides information on the activities to be carried out, the way in which it raises money and the administration and expenditure of the assets?
- Does the organisation not maintain more property that is reasonably required for the continuity of its public benefit activities?
- Do the organisational documents provide that any surplus in case of the organisation's liquidation is destined for a (similar) public interest?
- Have both the organisation and its board members, supervisory board members, management and other leading persons avoided any claims inciting persons to hatred or violence or the use of violence in the past four years?

In addition, the charity must publish its annual figures and its policy plan on its website. By way of exception, an endowed family charity need not publish its wealth, but merely a declaration of proceeds and expenditures. This is because the transparency requirements are politically motivated and are primarily targeted at fundraising charities.

## 3. Key comparative notes for family charities

### 3.1 Possibility of exit

For a charity to qualify as such, it is sometimes required that funds be transferred unconditionally to the charity. This is the case in Switzerland, for example. This makes a Swiss-based family charity vulnerable to legal or other objective changes. In Dutch practice, substantial gifts or endowments to a charity commonly contain conditional elements based on external circumstances such as negative tax developments affecting charities. For an international family, a possible exit should always be considered – especially since democracies generally tend to become more stringent with regard to the practice of charitable organisations.

### 3.2 Default without special tax status

A family should always consider what the default position would be in a jurisdiction. In fact, this should be the first question they consider. Depending on the purpose and ambitions of the family charity, whether it should apply for special tax status should also be determined. Increasingly, this does not appear to be necessary in the Netherlands. However, in many jurisdictions, a special tax status is required in order to receive gifts or generate investment income without effective taxation. In the Netherlands, there is no need for a special tax status in order to be exempt from corporate income tax with respect to all sorts of investments. The Netherlands' vast international treaty network should in principle apply to all foundations, whether they qualify for ANBI status or not.

The recognition of a charity implies a 'licence to operate', which goes further than mere compliance with the tax framework. In addition, where a charity has obtained ANBI status, it should be considered upfront what consequences and sanctions will arise upon its termination. This is an alternative to the issue of an exit. Currently, in the Netherlands, no direct sanctions apply on the loss of ANBI status.

**3.3 Bureaucracy**

In many sophisticated jurisdictions, charities must report annually and extensively to the tax authorities (and eventually also to the regulator, such as the Charity Commission in the United Kingdom) on their activities in the broadest sense. The Dutch approach is different and tends to be very practical, with no unnecessary red tape. Accordingly, there is no annual general reporting requirement for charities, but only an obligation to report on any material changes to the activities or intentions that may be relevant for ANBI qualification. As a consequence, ANBI status need not be renewed annually. Checks are carried out randomly and on the basis of risk factors. This is backed up by provisions in the tax law that empower the tax authorities to revoke ANBI status retroactively. This is an efficient system that functions quite well, with only approximately 45 civil servants controlling around 50,000 charities.

**3.4 Endowment and requisite expenditures**

In the context of tax qualification as a charity, most jurisdictions have specific requirements on the level of expenditure in support of a charitable cause. For example, US law has a 5% compulsory expenditure requirement for family charities, which may prove to be very cumbersome. The Dutch practice recognises that there is no 'one size fits all' and is thus of a more qualitative nature: a charity must make clear that it has a 'reasonable' policy regarding expenditure versus accumulation of assets in the context of the continuation of its public interest activities. In practice, a policy plan verifying the policies maintained in this respect substantiates this policy. If a grant contains specific guidance on the maintenance of the funds for the recipient organisation, the maintenance of the funds in accordance with this guidance is lawfully deemed to be 'reasonable'.

**3.5 Restrictions in competing with for-profits**

In nearly all jurisdictions, it is considered undesirable if non-profits compete with for-profit entities that are fully subject to tax. There are various ways to handle this 'non-compete' perspective. One way is to strictly forbid charities from owning a majority share in a for-profit entity, which is the case in the United States: the so-called 'excess business holding rules' provide a complex set of restrictions, breach of which will result in the imposition of severe sanctions on the charity and its board members. Increasingly, innovative charitable organisations that wish to make use of a parallel charitable and for-profit model look to jurisdictions other than the United States. All 'non-related' business income generated by a non-profit is subject to corporate tax in the United States.

In the Netherlands, there is full flexibility for charities to hold shares in for-profit entities. The non-compete issue is resolved in the Dutch context by the fact that for-profit activities are always subject to corporate income tax, even if they take place in a non-profit environment (and therefore, there is no distinction between (un)related business income). No restrictions in terms of the size and type of investments apply in the Dutch context; whereas in jurisdictions with more regulatory oversight, the rules of a 'prudent investor' must be followed, which usually means compulsory diversification of passive interests. For the more venture-type philanthropist, this may result in too serious a restriction.

**4. Final thoughts**

Increasingly, combinations of several distinct entities are being utilised, whereby a passive charity in a sophisticated regulated jurisdiction is combined with a generic foundation in another jurisdiction that offers more flexibility for venture-type investments. Also, a combination of

*"In nearly all jurisdictions, it is considered undesirable if non-profits compete with for-profit entities that are fully subject to tax."*

philanthropic and private activities may be structured in an alternate structure such as a 'private foundation' (not to be confused with the family charity in US terminology). The private foundation is very similar to a discretionary trust with mingled private and philanthropic purposes. If structured properly, these Dutch resident foundations are completely transparent for Dutch tax purposes and offer a solid wealth planning structure without adding tax costs for an international family.[4]

There are many variations on this theme, depending on the long-term vision of the family and how it should be governed into the future.

## Notes

1 See IA Koele, *International Taxation of Philanthropy* (International Bureau of Fiscal Documentation, 2007).
2 www.hudson.org/research/11363-index-of-philanthropic-freedom-2015.
3 In the United States, charities that are not supported by the public in large, but rather by an extended family or business are referred to as 'private foundations', which presents terminological issues given that the foundation as a legal form does not exist in the United States. The distinction between 'private' and 'public' – which, to the author's knowledge, is only found in the US legislation – is thus avoided.
4 Obviously, it should be verified how this structure would be viewed in their own jurisdiction. For more, see IA Koele, "The Dutch Private Foundation: a robust but flexible tool in dynastic structuring' in *Trusts & Trustees* (Oxford University Press, 2014); and IA Koele, "The Dutch Private Foundation in comparison with trusts: for the same purpose but rather different", *Trusts & Trustee*s (February 2016), www.koeletaxlegal.com/publications.

# VI. Caribbean choices

**Vanessa L Schrum**
Appleby (Bermuda) Limited

## 1. Introduction

The global impact and uncertainty brought about by the recent pandemic have highlighted the need for sound charitable and philanthropic structures. Many of these are being established by private clients to support worthy causes that resonate with them, with missions to cover health, education, wildlife, the environment and more. Often these philanthropic endeavours are arranged in a socially responsible manner, with a focus on impact and sustainability. To achieve these goals, clients are turning to structuring options in the Caribbean region for bespoke charitable and philanthropic giving. Many jurisdictions offer a selection of corporate vehicles and trusts, including charitable and non-charitable purpose trusts. The corporate vehicle is possibly the most familiar to many and offers members a structured forum for participation with added protection from personal liability. The trust structure, on the other hand, gives scope for creativity and can be adapted to changing circumstances. Arguably, a trust offers more privacy and centralised decision making. A few jurisdictions now offer foundations which may be used as not-for-profit enterprises. Some jurisdictions allow for the establishment of private trust companies, which often feature in a family's structure designed for philanthropic giving.

In this chapter, we will focus primarily on the structuring options available in Bermuda, the British Virgin Islands (BVI) and the Cayman Islands. All of these jurisdictions are tax neutral and have stable governments, favourable but well-respected regulatory regimes and robust professional services industries.

## 2. Bermuda

As a British overseas territory, Bermuda has a reliable legal system based on English common law, supplemented by a modern and commercial statutory framework and case law. It has a leading offshore insurance and reinsurance industry. Charitable and philanthropic structures commonly found in Bermuda include charitable trusts, purpose trusts and companies limited by guarantee. Unincorporated associations and charitable entities incorporated by private acts of Parliament are also possible, but perhaps less common.

### 2.1 Charitable purpose

The Charities Act[1] defines 'charitable purpose' to include any of the following, provided that it is for the public benefit:

- the prevention or relief of poverty;
- the advancement of education, religion, health or the saving of lives, citizenship or community development, arts, culture, heritage or science, sport, human rights, conflict resolution or reconciliation (or the promotion of religious or racial harmony or equality and diversity), environmental protection or improvement, or animal welfare;
- the relief of those in need because of youth, age, ill health, disability, financial hardship or other disadvantage;
- the promotion of the efficiency of the armed forces of the Crown, police, fire, rescue or ambulance services; and
- the provision of recreational and similar facilities in the interests of social welfare.

The 'public benefit' requirement is broken down into three distinct aspects:

- There must be an actual benefit to the public;
- Charities must serve the public or a sufficient section of the public, and must not unduly restrict access to their benefits; and
- Private or personal benefits must be necessary or incidental to achieving charitable purposes.

### 2.2 Registration as a Bermuda charity[2]

To be a Bermuda charity, an organisation must:

- be subject to the jurisdiction of the Bermuda Supreme Court; and

- have only 'charitable purposes' which must satisfy the 'public benefit' requirement.

The Charities Act requires every Bermuda charity to be registered[3] as a public charity or a privately funded charity, unless:

- it is exempt by regulations made by the registrar general acting on behalf of the charity commissioners; or
- it is privately funded and does not solicit funds from the Bermuda public, or receive funding from the Bermuda government or Bermuda public sources; and
  - in the case of a trust, has a licensed trustee[4] or private trust company as trustee; or
  - in the case of a guarantee company, has a registered office with, and is subject to compliance by, a Bermuda-regulated institution; and in each case
  - is exempted from registration by the charity commissioners.

All registered charities must prepare statements of accounts and annual reports to be submitted to the registrar general within six months of the end of the financial year. Accounting records and annual reports must be preserved for at least seven years.

*"As a British overseas territory, Bermuda has a reliable legal system based on English common law, supplemented by a modern and commercial statutory framework and case law."*

The register of public charities is open to public inspection together with all documents lodged in accordance with the provisions of the Charities Act. However, the register of privately funded charities together with its documents lodged with the registrar general is not open to public inspection and all documents so lodged are private.

### 2.3 Charitable trusts

Charitable trusts are established for exclusively charitable purposes and may be designed to continue indefinitely. While not a requirement, generally the sole trustee or one of the trustees will be a Bermuda licensed trust company in order to be considered exempt from the registration requirements specified above.

Trustees are regulated by the Bermuda Monetary Authority under the Trusts (Regulation of Trust Business) Act 2001. Regulation of trustees is also achieved through Bermuda's anti-money laundering and anti-terrorist financing legislation. The responsibility for enforcement rests with the attorney general, acting in the public interest. In contrast to a private trust, there are no beneficiaries who can apply to the court for enforcement. Regulation of charities registered under the Charities Act rests with the registrar general and the charity commissioners.

Bermuda has a stamp duty regime; but there is no duty on the document creating a trust, charitable or not, where:

- the trustee is a Bermuda licensed trust company and the trust property is non-Bermuda property (which includes foreign securities and foreign currency bank balances); or
- the trustee is an exempted company.

In the case of a registered charitable trust, the Charities Act requires that the charitable trust have an express dissolution clause providing that the trust assets will be applied for the purposes of the charity on termination of the trust.

### 2.4 Purpose trusts

The concept of the non-charitable purpose trust is a solution whereby the purposes of the trust or some of them do not meet the criteria for what is 'charitable' under Bermuda law (eg, to further the cause of a political party or to promote a non-charitable ideology). Bermuda was one of the first offshore jurisdictions to introduce non-charitable purpose trusts under legislation passed in 1989.[5]

**Table 1. Characteristics of a Bermuda purpose trust**

| | |
|---|---|
| **Creation** | In writing, usually by way of declaration made by the trustee. |
| **Duration** | May last indefinitely or for a specified term of years. |
| **Purpose** | Any purpose which is:<br><br>• sufficiently certain to allow the trust to be carried out;<br>• lawful; and<br>• not contrary to public policy. |
| **Trustee** | Usually a licensed trust company, but there are no special requirements or qualifications. |
| **Enforcement** | Any of the following persons has the right to apply to the court to enforce the trust:<br><br>• the settlor or grantor, unless the trust document says otherwise;<br>• the person, if any, appointed in the trust document (the so-called 'enforcer');<br>• a trustee; and<br>• any other person who the court considers has sufficient interest in the trust.<br><br>If none of the above is able and willing to do so, the attorney general may apply. The appointment of an enforcer is optional. Sometimes the enforcer is given additional powers, such as the power to appoint and remove trustees. |
| **Trust fund** | The trust fund may consist of cash or other investments; or could, for example, comprise the share capital of a special purpose vehicle. A purpose trust cannot hold Bermuda real property, but it may hold an interest in a company, partnership or other entity that does. |

## 2.5 Trust considerations

There are many advantages of using a charitable or purpose trust structure:

- Regulation: Trusts are unregulated unless registered in Bermuda and therefore have fewer regulatory requirements than charitable companies limited by guarantee, which are subject to the additional requirements of the Bermuda Companies Act 1981.
- Formation time: A trust can generally be established very quickly and subsequently registered if necessary.
- Flexibility: Where trust instruments provide for variation, trusts can be very flexible vehicles that can adapt to changing circumstances and stay current. The trustees can be empowered to:
  - hold property;
  - raise funds to meet the objectives of the organisation stated in the trust deed;
  - take legal advice;
  - borrow money; or
  - enter into any form of contract in the name of the trustees.
- Costs: No annual government or licence fees make trusts relatively inexpensive options. The costs to administer may vary and there is a nominal annual fee for registered charities.
- Beneficiaries: Trustees of a discretionary trust have full discretion as to which beneficiaries receive which capital or income, if any.
- Liability: Typically, the trust instrument will provide for trustee indemnification for breach of trust to avoid personal liability issues.
- Privacy: Documents lodged with the registrar general with respect to privately funded trusts are not available to members of the public and the Public Access to Information Act 2010 does not apply.
- Duration: A charitable or non-charitable purpose trust can last in perpetuity.

## 2.6 Companies limited by guarantee

A company limited by guarantee is well suited to collective and active enterprises. It is formed by one or more members who subscribe their names to the memorandum of association. The members are required to contribute to the assets of the guarantee company, but only to the extent of the guarantee fund. In Bermuda, a company limited by guarantee can be formed as a non-profit only if:

- its purpose is to promote art, science, religion, charity, sport, education or any other social or useful purpose; and
- its profit and income are used exclusively for charitable purposes.

*"A company limited by guarantee is well suited to collective and active enterprises. It is formed by one or more members who subscribe their names to the memorandum of association."*

No dividends may be paid to its members. Companies limited by guarantee are exempt from all annual taxes.

The memorandum of association for a guarantee company must state, among other things, that:

- the liability of its members is limited; and
- each member undertakes to contribute:
  - to the assets of the guarantee company in the event of it being wound up while he or she is a member or within one year after he or she ceases to be a member;
  - for the payment of the debts and liabilities of the company contracted before he or she ceases to be a member;
  - to the costs and charges and expenses of winding up; and
  - for the adjustment of the rights of the contributories among themselves,

such amount as may be required, not exceeding a specified amount.

All income of and property of the guarantee company must be applied solely towards the promotion of its objects as set out in the memorandum of association; and no portion thereof shall be paid or transferred directly or indirectly by way of dividend, bonus or otherwise by way of profit to the members of the guarantee company. If, upon winding up, there remains, after the satisfaction of all debts and liabilities of the guarantee company, any property, it shall not be paid to or distributed among the members of the guarantee company but shall be given to, or transferred to, some other charitable body or bodies having objects similar to those of the guarantee company.

The benefits of the corporate structure are as follows:

- Participation: It involves officers, committee members and members appointed democratically.
- Flexibility: It provides for flexibility and growth. Where provided for in the company bylaws, amendments to governance can be straightforward and relatively inexpensive.
- Formation time: A company limited by guarantee can be incorporated in a matter of days (provided that compliance information is forthcoming on a timely basis).
- Legal powers: A company has its own legal personality and undertakes all activities in its own name.
- Privacy: Incorporated companies must submit relevant incorporation information to the registrar of companies along with an annual updated register of members. While these are

*"The general principles of BVI law are derived from those of English law, supplemented by statute. Charitable and philanthropic structures commonly found in BVI include trusts (charitable, purpose and VISTA), and companies."*

unlikely to be overly revealing of any confidential information, this represents (marginally) less privacy than the Bermuda trust.
- Liability: The members of a company limited by guarantee are liable only for the amount contributed in the guarantee fund (usually a nominal sum such as $100), providing robust protection from personal liability for the members and governing board.
- Duration: Companies limited by guarantee can exist in perpetuity and may be dissolved only through a legal process known as winding up.

**3. British Virgin Islands**
The BVI is a British overseas territory. It is a popular jurisdiction for the use of corporate and holding structures. The general principles of BVI law are derived from those of English law, supplemented by statute. Charitable and philanthropic structures commonly found in BVI include trusts (charitable, purpose and VISTA), and companies. Charities can also be formed as unincorporated associations, assuming that the rules provide for a *cy-près* distribution (as near as possible to the donor's intention) on dissolution rather than a payment to members. Currently there is no foundation legislation in the BVI.

3.1 Charitable trusts
The principal legislation applicable to BVI trusts is the BVI Trustee Act 1961 (as amended). This is largely based on the English Trustee Act 1975. BVI law allows for the establishment of a trust to create a charitable fund or to make provision for existing charitable institutions or purposes.

A trust under BVI law is charitable if its purposes fall exclusively within one or more of the following categories of charitable purposes recognised by law and there is an element of public benefit:

- the relief of poverty;
- the advancement of education;
- the advancement of religion; or
- other purposes beneficial to the community as a whole.

A charitable trust can continue indefinitely.

The Non-Profit Organisation Act 2012 provides a framework for regulating charities and other non-profit organisations which operate predominantly in the BVI. The regime does not apply to:

- entities that are licensed under the Banks and Trust Companies Act 1990; or
- purpose trusts where the trustee is licensed under the Banks and Trust Companies Act 1990.

The Non-Profit Organisation Act applies to organisations engaged in the promotion of charitable, religious, cultural, educational, social or paternal purposes, or other activities or programmes for the benefit of the public, or a section of the public. Relevant organisations must:

- register with the Non-Profit Organisation Registration Board through the registrar of non-profit organisations;
- adhere to minimum establishment and annual reporting requirements; and
- remain subject to supervision and monitoring.

Reserved powers trusts are also permitted under BVI law where a settlor wishes to retain a certain level of control over specific elements of the administration of a trust (although care should be taken to ensure that there are no adverse tax or other consequences in doing so), or reserve such powers in favour of another. In this manner, certain powers that would usually be vested in the trustee can be conferred on a third-party 'protector', who can be an individual, a committee of individuals or a company. Such powers might include:

- changing the governing law;
- changing trustees;
- agreeing trustee fees;
- consenting to the change of beneficiaries; or
- approving distributions.

The BVI is one of a handful of jurisdictions that have given statutory recognition to the office of protector. It is not strictly necessary to include a protector of a BVI trust, but the appointment of a protector can be of benefit to oversee the fiduciary and discretionary powers of trustees and to ensure that any wishes of the settlor are properly considered.

**3.2 Purpose trusts**

Statutory non-charitable purpose trusts may be established in the BVI and can be used for philanthropic activities. Not being exclusively charitable trusts, they may benefit persons and/or further purposes, whether charitable or not. The following criteria concerning the purposes and trustee must be met.

**Table 2. Characteristics of a BVI purpose trust**

| | |
|---|---|
| **Duration** | May last indefinitely or for a specified term of years. |
| **Purpose** | Any purpose which is specific, reasonable and possible. The purpose must not be immoral, contrary to BVI public policy or unlawful. |
| **Trustee** | At least one trustee must be a 'designated person' (which usually results in the trustee being a licensed BVI trust company or a BVI private trust company). |
| **Enforcement** | At least one enforcer appointed in the trust deed must have exclusive standing to enforce the trust. |
| **Accounts** | There is a statutory obligation to keep accounts of the trust within the BVI in the case of a non-charitable purpose trust. |

### 3.3 VISTA

Perhaps the most popular form of trust vehicle in the BVI is one established under the Virgin Islands Special Trusts Act, 2003 (VISTA). This regime was designed to allow trusts of BVI shares to be created where the trustee is disengaged from administrative and management responsibilities for the affairs of that BVI company (and by extension, any company held below that BVI company). It allows the company and its business to be retained and run as its directors see fit. VISTA was specifically developed to act as a commercial trust vehicle and to avoid the traditional 'prudent man of business' rule, which restricted a trustee's options and was viewed as being undesirable in the modern commercial context. While a VISTA trust is particularly well suited for holding voting shares of funds, special purpose vehicles and other structured finance vehicles, it can also apply to charitable trusts or purpose trusts as long as certain conditions are satisfied.

The trustee of a VISTA trust must be a company which holds a licence to carry on trust business in the British Virgin Islands. The trustee of a VISTA trust may not be a director of the company.

VISTA allows the indefinite retention of the shares of a company and separates the trustee from the responsibility of management in a number of ways. The shares that form part of a VISTA trust must be specifically designated as such and will be held on 'trust to retain'. The trustee's primary responsibility will be to retain these shares as

*"The trustee's fiduciary obligations and duty of care regarding the assets of the trust or the conduct of the affairs of the company are restricted to an 'intervention call' on behalf of a beneficiary, parent or guardian or other interested person."*

part of the trust fund; and a trustee is no longer bound to preserve or enhance the value of the shares. The trustee is not accountable for losses arising, whether directly or indirectly, from holding rather than disposing of the shares. The trustee's fiduciary obligations and duty of care regarding the assets of the trust or the conduct of the affairs of the company are restricted to an 'intervention call' on behalf of a beneficiary, parent or guardian or other interested person.

The settlor of a VISTA trust may, via the trust instrument, create special rules relating to the office of director by providing the manner in which the trustee must exercise its voting powers in relation to the appointment, removal and remuneration of directors. Persons who act as director are absolved from a fiduciary duty under the trust (but VISTA does not remove a director's fiduciary duty to the company). The sale of shares in a company is prohibited without the approval of the directors or such other persons as are specified in the trust instrument. Where specifically expressly excluded by the trust instrument, the rule in *Saunders v Vautier* will not apply for up to a maximum of 20 years (or such shorter period as may be set out in the trust deed) to a VISTA trust. The trust instrument may also provide that the terms of VISTA will apply to some, but not all, of the shares designated to the trust.

### 3.4 Companies

As above, typically these are formed as companies limited by guarantee so that the members will not be entitled to any profits or surplus on dissolution.

## 4. Cayman Islands

The Cayman Islands is a British overseas territory. It is a popular jurisdiction for international funds. The general principles of Cayman law are derived from those of English common law, with its own local statutes and case decisions of the Grand Court, of which there is a dedicated Financial Services Division. Charitable and philanthropic structures commonly found in Cayman include:

- charitable trusts;
- the STAR regime (non-charitable purpose trusts);
- foundation companies;
- private family funds;
- companies; and
- unincorporated associations (assuming that the rules provide for a *cy-près* or as near as possible distribution on dissolution rather than a distribution to members beneficially).

The Non-Profit Organisations Law (2020 Revision)[6] provides a framework for regulating charities and other non-profit organisations operating primarily in Cayman. This law impacts any company, trust or other body of persons that:

- solicits contributions from the public; and
- is established primarily for the promotion of charitable purposes or activities.[7]

The law does not apply to:

- entities licensed under the Banks and Trust Companies Law (2020 Revision);
- government entities;
- non-profit organisations that are designated non-financial businesses or professions registered under the Anti-Money Laundering Regulations (2020 Revision); or
- non-profit organisations registered or holding a licence under any of the regulatory laws, other than entities registered as an excluded person under Section 5(4) of the Securities Investment Business Law (2020 Revision).

Relevant organisations must register with the registrar of non-profit organisations. The law gives public access to certain information about charities and their management teams through the establishment of the non-profit organisations register. The registered charity must file annual returns and keep financial statements.

**4.1 Charitable trusts**
As above, trusts formed for charitable purposes are also common in Cayman. A trust continues to be an extremely flexible planning tool.

**4.2 STAR regime (purpose trust)**
Part VIII of the Trusts Law (2020 Revision) (STAR Act)[8] allows for the creation of a non-charitable purpose trust and other special trusts and powers under Cayman Islands law. STAR is unique to the Cayman Islands and applies only where the trust instrument contains a declaration to that effect. It allows Cayman trusts to be created for philanthropic purposes which are outside of the scope of what would be considered charitable as a matter of Cayman Islands law.

Before the enactment of the STAR Act, it was not possible to create trusts for a purpose other than a 'charitable purpose' (as defined under the law of England and Wales). The STAR Act was passed in response to the popular demand for private purpose trusts. The major rules militating against purpose trusts were overcome by the STAR Act, which provides a secure legal framework for purpose trusts. For example, the beneficiary principle (which provides that there must be an ascertainable beneficiary with a proprietary interest in the trust property capable of enforcing the trust) has been overcome by the designation of an enforcer who is subject to fiduciary duties. The requirement of certainty, whereby the terms of the trust must be sufficiently clear and capable of being executed, is facilitated in the STAR Act by giving the court the power to resolve uncertainty. A purpose trust may be perpetual, unless the purpose trust is deemed to be contrary to public policy. The STAR Act also gives the court the power to resolve any uncertainty as to the objects or administration of the trust.

The STAR Act is not just restricted to non-charitable purpose trusts and can be invoked by the settlor to cover trusts of all kinds, such as:

- trusts for persons;
- trusts for purposes (charitable or non-charitable); and
- trusts for a combination of persons and purposes.

This provides for planning flexibility for settlors.

**Table 3. Characteristics of a purpose trust established under the STAR Act**

| | |
|---|---|
| **Creation** | A trust or power which is subject to the STAR Act must:<br><br>• be in writing, either testamentary or *inter vivos*; and<br>• contain a declaration that the STAR Act is to apply or, if there is no such declaration, the STAR Act must otherwise be deemed to apply. |
| **Duration** | May be perpetual, unless the purpose trust is deemed contrary to public policy. |
| **Objects and purposes** | The objects or beneficiaries can be persons of any number and/or purposes of any number or kind, charitable or non-charitable, provided that such purposes are lawful and not contrary to public policy. |
| **Trustee** | A trust company licensed in the Cayman Islands under the Bank and Trusts Companies Act (Revised), as amended from time to time, or a private trust company registered in the Cayman Islands, must be the trustee or co-trustee. |
| **Enforcement** | There must be one or more enforcers, who may or may not be beneficiaries, appointed under the terms of the trust document or by court order (eg, where the enforcer under the trust document is unable or unwilling to act, or if there is no enforcer for any reason). A beneficiary has no standing as such to enforce the trust, which right is vested in the enforcer. A beneficiary has no information rights. |
| **Trust fund** | The trust fund may consist of cash or other investments. A STAR trust cannot hold land in the Cayman Islands, but may hold an interest in a company, partnership or other entity which does. |

Purpose trusts have many useful applications. Settlors can create purpose trusts in cases where they are not certain that the purposes qualify as exclusively charitable. A purpose trust may be used for quasi-charitable trusts, with philanthropic or partly non-charitable purposes, given that many worthy causes are not necessarily charitable or wholly charitable. A purpose trust may also be used where, for example, the settlor wants to benefit his or her family, but also wants to ensure the continuation of the family business. As a beneficiary of a purpose trust has no standing to enforce the trust, the settlor's wishes cannot be overridden by the beneficiaries when they are all adults.[9]

There is no requirement to register a STAR trust with the regulatory authorities in the Cayman Islands; hence, confidentiality is preserved. In fact, all trust deeds (except 'exempted trusts') are exempt from registration. Therefore, the details of a STAR trust will remain confidential, subject only to disclosure as may be required by an order of the Cayman Islands courts or under a tax information exchange agreement, properly invoked in accordance with its terms.

### 4.3 Companies

As above, typically these are companies limited by guarantee so that members have no entitlement to profits or surplus on dissolution.

### 4.4 Foundations

A relatively new private wealth vehicle now available in Cayman is the foundation company. Under the Cayman Foundation Companies Act, 2017,[10] a foundation company may be incorporated or an existing Cayman exempted company may be converted into a foundation company. The legislation is drafted to allow the foundation company to operate under Cayman Islands company law, having its own legal personality and transacting in its own right, but with characteristics and advantages of a trust. This may be attractive to individuals from civil law jurisdictions where trusts are unfamiliar or give rise to tax or reporting issues. While corporate in nature, often the governing documents will have features similar to a trust – for example, the role of the 'founder' who establishes the foundation company is somewhat similar to that of a settlor of a trust, having the ability to retain certain powers but carrying limited risk of challenge.

The law applies only to companies that have been declared by the registrar of companies to be foundation companies. Foundation companies do not need shareholders or members following incorporation, but must at all times have at least one supervisor (who may but need not be a director) and a secretary who is a 'qualified person'.[11] A foundation company is managed by its board of directors. A foundation company can be formed for any lawful purpose or purposes, including charitable and non-charitable purposes, and can be a highly flexible vehicle. It can hold property and can be used for a number of private client, family office and philanthropic objectives (which need not be beneficial to other persons).

## Notes

1 The Charities Act 2014, as amended by the Charities Amendment Act 2018.
2 An application to register as a charity, together with the charity trustee declaration, is both vetted by the charity commissioners, who are guided by the Charities Act, the Charities Regulations 2014 (Regulations) and the Charities (Anti-Money Laundering, Anti-Terrorist Financing and Reporting) Regulations 2014.
3 Registration may be indefinite or for a definite period of one, three or five years at a time. The Charities Act also allows for temporary three-month licences to solicit and collect donations in limited circumstances.
4 Being a Bermuda-regulated institution licensed under the Trusts (Regulation of Trust Business) Act 2001.
5 Part II of the Trusts (Special Provisions) Act 1989, as amended in 1998.
6 Introduced as part of the Cayman Islands implementation of Financial Action Task Force recommendations to facilitate the investigation and enforcement of anti-money laundering and terrorism financing.
7 The Non-Profit Organisations Law applies to organisations engaged in the promotion of charitable, religious, cultural, educational, social or paternal purposes, or other activities or programmes for the benefit of the public, or a section of the public within the Cayman Islands or elsewhere.
8 The concept of private purpose trusts was introduced into the Cayman Islands via the Special Trusts (Alternative Regime) Act 1997, now embedded in Part VIII of the Trusts Act.
9 Because the rule in *Saunders v Vautier* (1841) Cr 2 Ph 240 will not apply to a purpose trust.
10 2017 Revision, which came into force on 18 October 2017.
11 Someone who is licensed or permitted by Cayman's Companies Management Law (Revised) to provide company management services in Cayman.

# VII. How families use donor-advised funds and other giving vehicles

**Eileen R Heisman**
National Philanthropic Trust

## 1. Introduction

Philanthropy can be one of the most meaningful and deeply held values in a family. Charitable giving and acts of service can strengthen bonds, build legacies and highlight other important values, such as leadership and education. Like most multi-generational endeavours, family philanthropy is most rewarding – and most efficient – when it is strategically executed and involves family members in thoughtful ways.

Increasingly, family offices and other professional advisers are expanding their practices to include enhanced philanthropic services. These advisers recognise that effective family philanthropy requires a holistic approach and should be considered a part of total wealth management. Your family may feel passionate about your charitable giving goals, but may be uncertain of how to achieve them together or teach them to the next generation. You can find advisers with expertise in philanthropy as well as investing, succession planning and tax planning, all of which are highly relevant in creating a successful, strategic and long-term multi-generational giving plan.

In the United States, nearly 90% of high-net-worth households participate in charitable giving, compared to 41% of the general population.[1] Very often, family philanthropy utilises giving vehicles to streamline and maximise giving. Families with giving vehicles – such as donor-advised funds (DAFs), private family foundations and charitable trusts – are significantly more likely to have a philanthropic strategy in place.[2] These vehicles can be used independently or in tandem to help donors and their families to achieve their philanthropic vision.

This chapter provides an overview of charitable giving vehicles and focuses on DAFs – the most popular giving vehicle in the United States. It also describes the flexibility of DAFs to share and practise family philanthropy.

## 2. Why family philanthropy matters

Multi-generational philanthropy offers a powerful way for families to have an impact on their communities through the charitable organisations and causes that mean the most to them. Philanthropy can bring your family closer by creating shared experiences and practising shared values. It can strengthen and deepen family bonds.

### 2.1 Leaving a legacy

It is often said that 'philanthropy starts at home'. Like most values, a philanthropic spirit is often modelled by parents and grandparents and observed by their children. If sharing long-held values is linear from one generation to the next, the execution of philanthropy offers more opportunities to collaborate. Members of all generations can participate in philanthropy and can experience it through their own lens.

Family values are hugely important to younger generations. More than nine in 10 millennial and Generation Z children of high-net-worth parents say that the most important thing they will inherit from their parents is their values, not their wealth. Over 80% want to sustain and build on their family's legacy.[3] This indicates a strong commitment from the next generation to carry on family values through their philanthropy.

### 2.2 Engaging the next generation

Giving as a family affords younger generations a chance to influence family activities, such as which charitable causes the family supports. Two-thirds of high-net-worth families give together. However, only one-third of the children reported feeling that they have a strong voice in the family's philanthropy.[4] This data demonstrates an opportunity for families to more fully align – and potentially evolve – how they realise their collective philanthropic strategy.

Engaging the next generation – whether through understanding their motivations for giving or encouraging them to find their own charitable interests – is key to sustaining a family's philanthropic legacy. Older generations need to include the next generation by involving them in conversations about giving, such as how the family supports certain causes or the impacts of their past gifts. Giving histories are often points of pride or have deep emotional connections, which can offer a chance to strengthen family ties. There is also a tremendous benefit to discussing philanthropic strategies with younger generations. Emerging strategies, such as using online-accessible giving vehicles, can provide hands-on opportunities for younger generations to learn both the why and the how of their family's philanthropy.

**Philanthropy as a reflection of evolving values**

Increasingly, younger generations are finding charitable causes they care about, which may differ from a family's traditional giving history. Families can still forge a philanthropic path together by acknowledging the commonalities in the causes they care about.

As an example, one of our donor families at National Philanthropic Trust, a US donor-advised fund provider, shifted its giving strategy to include the children's philanthropic goals.

During Summer 2020, two generations of one family came together to address issues that reflect longstanding inequities. Historically, the parents had recommended grants to organisations that promoted gender diversity in specific industries. Influenced by the global reaction to the police brutality experienced by black people and other people of colour, the teenage daughters pushed to include racial equity as a focus in their family philanthropy. During their conversations about giving and charitable priorities, they recognised a shared commitment to inclusion and an opportunity to broaden their family's philanthropic mission. As a result, the donors began recommending grants to charitable organisations that combat racism and create systemic change within the justice system and beyond.

### 2.3 Philanthropic tools for families

There are many tools that families use to plan and practise philanthropy. Many engage professional advisers as an integral part of family philanthropic planning and execution, and to recommend the best tools to achieve their charitable goals. Their expertise can offer smart guidance on how families can maximise their philanthropic impact. For example, a financial or family office adviser can help philanthropists to assess which assets are the most tax advantageous for a charitable contribution. Alternatively, if a family wants to create a giving vehicle that will last in perpetuity, advisers can suggest which ones allow donors to 'pass down' the vehicle to the next generation. Professional advisers can also advise on how to invest charitable

*"Giving vehicles are a common way to structure a family's philanthropy. There are different types of giving vehicles that help families to accomplish their giving goals, including private family foundations, DAFs and charitable trusts."*

assets in a giving vehicle so that families can give consistently across generations.

Giving vehicles are a common way to structure a family's philanthropy. There are different types of giving vehicles that help families to accomplish their giving goals, including private family foundations, DAFs and charitable trusts. While each giving vehicle offers different advantages, all are designed to help families leave lasting philanthropic legacies.

**3. Choosing the right giving vehicle**
Giving vehicles are usually a central part of multi-generational philanthropy. They can provide efficiency and help to create a common understanding of what is – and is not – permissible. Private foundations and DAFs function in a similar fashion: you make irrevocable contributions to the giving vehicle, receive immediate tax deductions and use the charitable assets to make grants to qualified organisations. But the two giving vehicles also have important differences. You and your family must consider aspects such as contribution limits, legacy plans, fees, investments and donor control when choosing a vehicle for your family's philanthropy.

### 3.1 Donor-advised funds versus private foundations

In the United States, DAFs and private foundations are the two most commonly used giving vehicles. Details in this section are specific to US laws and taxation. DAFs and private foundations have similar goals, as both are structured vehicles for fulfilling a donor's philanthropic intent. However, the two are legally very different and each vehicle has different requirements, benefits and limitations.

One of the primary differences is how they are administered and by whom. Families that use private foundations are responsible for finding professional advisers, often lawyers, to establish the foundation. On an ongoing basis, the family is also responsible for due diligence, record keeping, accounting, reporting and tax filing. For this reason, most family foundations spend significant resources on external advisers, such as lawyers, accountants and financial advisers. Families that use DAFs to fulfil their charitable giving goals do not perform – or need to outsource – any of this administrative work. The DAF sponsoring organisation performs all of it. The cost of starting and maintaining a DAF is typically much lower than the cost of establishing and operating a private foundation.

Advisory privileges are another difference between DAFs and other charitable giving vehicles. Private foundations allow donors full control over grant recipients and investment strategies. With a DAF, donors may advise how the DAF charitable assets are used from both investment and grant-making perspectives by providing non-binding recommendations to the DAF sponsor, but the DAF sponsor makes the final decision. Many DAF sponsors offer multiple pre-approved investment options and some allow for custom investments subject to approval.

Finally, privacy is another key distinction. Details about private foundations, such as grant-making activity, expenses and board members, are publicly available as part of their annual tax filings with the Internal Revenue Service (IRS). DAF sponsors also file information returns with the IRS, but report their activity in the aggregate. This affords individual donors full anonymity. (DAF donors may recommend grants anonymously as well, although the vast majority elect to include their name(s) on the grant cheque, allowing the recipient charity to know the identity of the donor.)

There are other important distinctions, such as tax benefits and legally required minimum annual distributions. For a look at other similarities and differences between DAFs and private foundations, see Table 1.

**Table 1. Donor-advised funds versus private foundations**

| | Donor-advised funds | Private foundations |
|---|---|---|
| **Start-up time** | Immediate | Can take several weeks or months |
| **Start-up costs** | None | Legal (and other) fees are typically substantial |
| **Ongoing administrative and management fees** | 85 basis points (0.85%) or less, plus investment management fees | Can be in the range of 250-400 basis points (2.5% to 4% per year) |
| **Tax deduction limits for gifts of cash of stock or real property** | 60% of adjusted gross income | 30% of adjusted gross income |
| **Tax deduction limits for gifts** | 30% of adjusted gross income | 20% of adjusted gross income |
| **Valuation of gifts** | Fair market value* | Fair market value* for publicly traded stock, cost basis for all other gifts, including gifts of closely held stock or real property |
| **Required grant distribution** | None | Must distribute 5% of net asset value annually |
| **Excise tax on investment income** | None | Excise tax on 1.39% of net investment income annually |
| **Privacy** | Names of individual donors are not disclosed to the public, and grants can be made anonymously | Must file informational returns, which are available to the general public, disclosing detailed information on grants, investment fees, trustee names, staff salaries, etc. |
| **Administrative responsibilities** | Recommend grants to favourite charitable causes | Manage assets, keep records, select charities, administer grants, file state and federal tax returns, maintain board minutes, etc. |

**Fair market valuation of gifts is for assets held longer than one year.*
*Source: National Philanthropic Trust.*

**Creating a family giving plan**

The first step of family philanthropy is to create a family giving strategy. When creating a philanthropic strategy, families and their advisers can start with the following steps to ensure an effective giving plan and positive experience:

- Start the dialogue: From the outset, commit to having productive conversations about giving as a family. Family philanthropy is not always easy, but it is important to discuss everything together – whether that is which charitable causes to support or how to invest for future grant making. Maintaining open-mindedness, listening and working to find similarities in any differences (eg, do different causes have geography in common?) can keep conversations on track. Many families use outside consultants to convene these conversations.
- Strategise: Create the framework and goals for family philanthropy. A successful strategy can serve as a roadmap for the process and a reminder of overarching goals. Families should:
  - align their goals;
  - decide on which giving vehicle(s) to use;
  - agree on a decision-making structure and how to manage the budget; and
  - create a succession plan.

It's also important to build flexibility into all aspects of your philanthropic strategy. Acknowledge that your strategy reflects your family's current priorities and consider the ways it can evolve as social problems, the way they get addressed and the next generation's interests evolve.

- Use external resources: Remember that you can call in professionals if needed on any aspect of philanthropic work. Attorneys and estate planners can help you to choose the right vehicle for your family. Financial advisers can help you to consider your long and short-term investment strategy based on your grant-making goals. Consider consulting with your accountant on the most tax-efficient assets to donate. Philanthropic experts can guide conversations so that they keep the big picture giving goals in focus. Many DAF providers offer materials on how to use giving vehicles to maximise philanthropy. External advisers also stay current and can advise on the newest trends, tools or legal changes that impact philanthropy. Engaging these experts every few years can ensure that you are using the most effective philanthropic strategies. It's also important for donors to stay current on philanthropic topics of interests. Families can attend conferences, join webinars and subscribe to philanthropic trade publications. There are also philanthropic associations designed to help and bring together families with philanthropic interests so that they can learn from one another.

- Evaluate your efforts: The work of philanthropy is often a lifelong journey. It's important to regularly assess your charitable giving and impact, and the strategies you use:
  - Have your philanthropic goals stayed the same or evolved?
  - Do you have the capacity to make more grants to new charities or grant more money to the same charities?
  - Are your grants having the desired impact?
  - Are your investments supporting your grant-making timeline?
  - Should you consider aligning your investments with your philanthropic values through impact investing?
  - Is it time to add or pivot to the next generation's interests and leverage the flexibility you built into your strategy to allow for more personal philanthropy?

These are all questions to ask and answer each year to ensure that your family's philanthropy is as effective and impactful as you want it to be.

- Realign: It is important to consider how and when your family may want to evolve your philanthropy. Change is a normal part of family life and philanthropy should also change to reflect the times, tools and practices in which it is happening. Keeping an open mind and an open dialogue about philanthropy within your family can help that evolution to feel natural. The realignment phase is exactly why your family should build flexibility into its plan from the outset. Giving goals should be adaptable. Regardless of the timeframe you analyse, the next generation's social, economic and environmental issues are different from the preceding generations. Tools such as giving vehicles and impact investments can change. When you give your family permission to embrace new organisations, emerging issues and new solutions, they feel ownership of the philanthropic strategy. Embrace the process.

**4. More about DAFs**

DAFs are the fastest-growing philanthropic vehicle in the United States. The number of DAFs exceeds private foundations by nearly 10:1, but private foundations hold significantly more assets than DAFs. Below we explore how and why DAFs have become so popular.

4.1 A brief history of DAFs

DAFs were first established at charitable community foundations in the United States in the 1930s. DAFs were little-known giving vehicles for more than 50 years, but have more recently experienced explosive growth. In the mid-1990s, financial institutions began launching their own charities to offer DAFs, changing the trajectory of DAF growth. Today, there are more than one million individual DAF accounts in the United States that hold nearly $160 billion in charitable assets. The latter figure is an 84% increase in the last five years alone.[5] See Figure 1 to view the past decade of growth in DAF charitable assets.

**Figure 1. Total assets in DAFs ($ billions)**

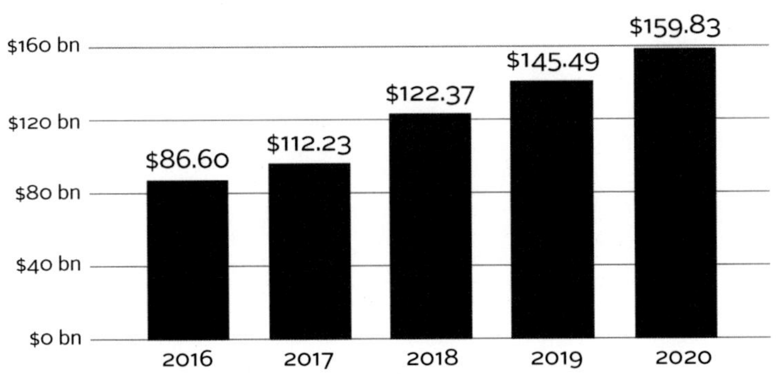


DAFs are also gaining popularity in other countries, such as the United Kingdom, where charitable assets in DAFs have increased almost 75% in the last five years alone, from £988 million to £1.7 billion.[6]

4.2 How DAFs work

To understand why DAFs have become so popular, it is important to understand how they work:

- Establishing the DAF: First, an individual, family, corporation or other entity establishes a DAF at a public charity, also known as the donor-advised fund charitable sponsor ('DAF sponsor'). The individual or entity that opens the DAF can designate the primary adviser – typically the same individual, a family member or representative. The primary adviser retains advisory privileges to the fund, such as:
  - appointing other advisers (including financial advisers);
  - recommending grants and investments; and
  - establishing a succession plan.

*"More than 1,000 organisations in the United States sponsor DAFs. They range in mission and size. From large financial institutions to small local community foundations, the varied identities of DAF sponsors often inform key policies and programmes for donors."*

Generally, the primary adviser is also the donor; but sometimes other outside parties may make contributions or may be given advisory privileges on the DAF.

- Contributing to the DAF: After the DAF is established, the donor makes an irrevocable contribution for which they can claim an immediate tax deduction. Some DAF sponsors have low or no minimum contribution thresholds, while others have $10,000 or more as an initial contribution requirement. DAF donors can claim immediate tax deductions for each additional contribution to the DAF. Most DAF sponsors accept commonly held assets such as cash and publicly traded securities. While some DAF sponsors only accept these more common assets, others also accept complex assets such as real estate, collections, cryptocurrencies or restricted stock.
- Granting from the DAF: Once the DAF is funded, the adviser(s) may recommend grants to charities from the DAF assets. The DAF sponsor performs all due diligence to ensure that the recipients are all qualified charitable organisations and that the grant will be used for permissible purposes. The DAF sponsor processes all grant recommendations, sends the grant cheques to recipient charities and maintains all of the records.

- Investing for future philanthropy: The DAF advisers may also recommend investment strategies for the DAF's charitable assets. Most DAF sponsors offer a pre-approved menu of investments that satisfy donors' varied risk tolerances and expected grant-making horizons. Others allow the advisers to recommend custom investments – usually when the DAF account balance is above a certain threshold. In all cases, advisers have only advisory privileges – hence the name 'donor-advised fund' – and the DAF sponsor must review and approve each grant and investment recommendation.

A simplified chart that demonstrates how DAFs work is shown in Figure 2.

**Figure 2. How DAFs work**

**Choosing a DAF sponsor**

More than 1,000 organisations in the United States sponsor DAFs. They range in mission and size. From large financial institutions to small local community foundations, the varied identities of DAF sponsors often inform key policies and programmes for donors.

When deciding where to establish a DAF, it is important to ask the DAF sponsor key questions. DAF sponsors have different policies that may influence where a family wants to establish a DAF. Families should find answers to the following questions:

- Legacy: What are my succession plan options? Some DAF sponsors limit the number of generations that may advise the DAF or require that the balance be granted to a charitable organisation after only one generation; while others allow donors to appoint successors so the DAF may exist in perpetuity.
- Investing: What are my investment options? Each DAF sponsor has its own investment policy guidelines. Custom investment plans or impact investing may be important to a family, so it is critical to confirm the investment options before opening the DAF.

- Contributions: What assets does the DAF sponsor accept? Like investments, each DAF sponsor has its own gift acceptance policies and procedures. Some will only take liquid assets, while others accept complex assets. If a family has a diverse portfolio that they want to turn into philanthropic support, they should ensure that the DAF sponsor can capably accept and liquidate their assets.
- Fees: What fees does the sponsor charge? Each DAF sponsor sets its own fee schedules. Most administrative fees are based on DAF asset balances, but others have flat fees. Investment selection also carries its own fees and some DAF sponsors can compensate financial advisers for their investment services. It is hugely important to understand the fees that each DAF sponsor charges before establishing your DAF.
- Point of view: Does the DAF sponsor's mission align with my own values? Some DAF sponsors have specific issues or geographic areas that they are designed to support. For example, a college or university may have a DAF programme that requires a certain percentage of each DAF contribution to go to a designated purpose or fund at the school. Similarly, a religiously affiliated DAF sponsor may only allow donors to support causes that align with their religious beliefs. Community foundations are intended to serve specific areas, whether a single metropolitan area or a region, and often have programmes to support their communities. Ensure that your DAF sponsor's mission enables your giving priorities.
- Accessibility: Can I manage my DAF online? Technology has moved our lives online rapidly. It can help us give to charity in just a few clicks, enabling faster support – often when charities need it most. Determine whether a DAF sponsor's technology allows you to open your DAF, contribute to it and recommend grants from it online; and whether that accessibility is important to you or your family members who may help advise the DAF.

A DAF sponsor's policies play an integral role in how families use their DAF to reach their giving goals.

**5. How families use DAFs**

As DAFs grow in popularity, families are adopting them to execute their multi-generational giving. The ways in which they use DAFs are almost as varied as the families themselves. What follows are several real-life examples of philanthropic families with DAFs at National Philanthropic Trust. These stories highlight the flexible ways they use DAFs to realise their individual and collective charitable goals.

### 5.1 Giving together and individually

Because DAFs allow for multiple advisers, they are an ideal giving vehicle for family philanthropy.

> *Three brothers – co-owners of a family business and all generous philanthropists – wanted a way to give as a family and honour their own individual philanthropic interests. To achieve this goal, each brother established his own DAF to support causes that resonated with him personally. Then, they established a fourth DAF where all three served as advisers. They used the 'family DAF' to experience giving as a family and to teach the next generation about their deeply held philanthropic values.*
>
> *Each brother had his own interest, along with his family's, in charitable organisations. One generously supported educational causes while another was deeply committed to healthcare. Their individual DAFs allowed them to contribute to their DAF when it made financial sense and recommend grants to whatever causes they choose, whenever they were moved to give. They used their family DAF to honour their parents and other loved ones, such as their childhood caregiver. The brothers regularly discussed their grant-making goals for the family DAF and had a strategic approach to making contributions to the DAF and recommending grants from it. An added benefit: each DAF had a customised succession plan so that their children, grandchildren and favourite charities would continue their legacies of giving. This family-minded structure leveraged the full flexibility of DAFs to support their giving goals.*

### 5.2 DAFs as a complement to private foundations

Many ultra-high-net-worth families utilise multiple giving vehicles and have both private family foundations and DAFs. The two vehicles offer different advantages and using them in tandem can maximise a family's robust philanthropy.

> *One family has a private foundation with a specific healthcare-related mission and a sophisticated approval process for grant-making. This structure helps them to be incredibly strategic and effective in their giving, but it does not offer family members with different interests much flexibility. When non-healthcare*

*related causes arise that they want to support, the family makes a grant from their private foundation to a DAF. Then, they use the DAF to support these 'off-mission' charitable organisations. DAFs can also be a great tool for young philanthropists who may wish to pursue charitable interests that differ from their family's philanthropic mission.*

Another strategy for coordinating giving between private foundations and DAFs is anonymity. Private foundations' activities are publicly disclosed in their tax filings. Using a DAF allows donors to remain anonymous if they wish.

*A family used both a private foundation and a DAF so that they could anonymously recommend grants to their children's schools. The family wanted to support the institutions with meaningful and impactful grants, but did not want the considerable attention this might bring to their family or their children. The donors made a grant from their private foundation to their DAF, then used the DAF to recommend a large grant to the schools anonymously. It should be noted: anonymous grants from DAFs are not common. In fact, at National Philanthropic Trust, less than 4% of grants are made anonymously. However, in certain circumstances, a family may value the ability to give without recognition, which is a feature that only DAFs can offer.*

### 5.3 International giving

Navigating international grant-making regulations and performing general due diligence for grants to charities in other countries can be complex and costly. DAF sponsors that make international grants help to streamline the process so that donors can focus on their giving.

One donor family immigrated to the US from India. Their family philanthropy focused largely on supporting charitable organisations in their home country. Using their DAF, they had several ways to accomplish their giving goals. They could recommend grants to US-based charities that work in India, to intermediary charities that are US-based and fund overseas charities or to charities based in India using one of two due diligence processes. The family used all three options on a regular basis to provide housing for elderly Indians living in poverty, address clean water access in rural Indian communities and provide proper nutrition for orphaned children in India.

### 5.4 Family legacies

As previously mentioned, DAFs offer many ways for families to engage the younger generations. DAFs can be hands-on tools for giving that help the youngest family members to better understand the importance of philanthropy.

*"Navigating international grant-making regulations and performing general due diligence for grants to charities in other countries can be complex and costly."*

A philanthropic couple passionately gave to arts organisations. They had no children and chose to involve their nieces and nephews in their giving. On every birthday, each child recommended a grant to a charity. The children did the research and suggested which organisation they wanted to support. Then the couple made a grant recommendation from their DAF to that charity in the child's honour. Together, they shared the communication from the charity so that the children saw how the grant benefited the community or cause, and more fully understood the importance of their personal philanthropy.

As they moved into retirement age, the donor couple considered the assets they wanted to use to fund their ongoing philanthropy. Having no heirs and a long-time dedication to the arts, they converted some of their most unique and complex assets – such as a collection of important antique furniture – into philanthropic assets by contributing them to the DAF sponsor and making grants from the proceeds after the assets were liquidated. The couple's succession plan was designed to support these charities after their lifetime.

**6. Conclusion**

As families consider their philanthropic strategy, they will notice how much giving is influenced by the times in which it exists. Family philanthropy too keeps evolving. There is no one right way to give, but philanthropic trends reflect shifting mindsets and tools. For example, the tradition of operating a family foundation in perpetuity is now competing with the rise of a 'giving while living' mindset. The onset of technology has helped philanthropists to move faster than ever. Not accidentally, the growth of DAFs has coincided with these trends because they are particularly flexible and can adapt to the changing needs of donors and their families.

Looking ahead, DAFs' growth trajectory will likely continue. Currently, DAF donors pay out around 20% of their charitable assets on an annual basis. This means that DAF donors are active and generous philanthropists (particularly when contrasted with the average 5% pay-out rate at private foundations). I predict that DAFs will be among the most sustainable forms of philanthropy. Grant making from DAFs is on the rise, growing on average 13% annually for the past several years. DAFs were one of the most generous sources of giving during the COVID-19 pandemic and other crises of 2020.

Charitable giving is one of humankind's oldest and most enduring traditions. Affluent families have long embraced philanthropy with enthusiasm and thoughtfulness. Even as giving becomes more globalised and uses more technology, it can still be inclusive for family members and can reflect a family's most deeply held values.

## Notes

1 Bank of America in partnership with the Indiana University Lilly Family School of Philanthropy, *The 2021 Bank of America Study of Philanthropy: Charitable Giving by Affluent Households* (2021).
2 *Ibid.*
3 Wells Fargo, *Children of Millionaires Survey*, 2019.
4 *Ibid.*
5 National Philanthropic Trust, *2021 Donor-Advised Fund Report.*
6 National Philanthropic Trust UK, *UK Donor-Advised Fund Report*, 2020.

# VIII. Women, philanthropy and the future of giving

**Kecia Barkawi**
VALUEworks

In 2009, I was asked by one of our clients – a female wealth owner – to support her in defining and implementing the strategy for her philanthropic activities. The journey with her and others in the years that followed has been a fascinating window on what giving can achieve in addressing global challenges. It has been a constant reminder of the critical role of philanthropy in promoting family cohesion and engaging the next generation. And it has been a continuous illustration of the inspirational leadership of women philanthropists in defining the future of giving – by giving early, giving collaboratively and giving strategically.

**1. Rising women's wealth and philanthropy**

Women's wealth is on the rise. Currently accounting for around one-third of total financial assets, women are estimated to add around $5 trillion of wealth each year. They are also projected to outgrow the global wealth pool in the years to come.[1] With more women in leadership positions than ever before and female entrepreneurship expanding, the wealth under the control of women continues to climb.[2] Demographics – in particular, the longer life expectancy of women compared to men – add to this development; and generational and spousal wealth transfers are further drivers.[3]

The trend is global, and it is here to stay. In the United States, women are expected to control much of the $30 trillion that baby boomers will possess by 2030.[4] In Asia, a new generation of women is transforming regional dynamics as more affluent, educated and empowered women come into the picture. And above-average growth of female wealth in Latin America, Eastern Europe, the Middle East and Africa is putting an increasing share of women in the driving seat of wealth decisions across the world.[5]

In parallel, the role of women in philanthropy leaves a growing imprint on giving worldwide. Gender matters in philanthropy. Men and women engage in philanthropy differently. One is not better than the other; they're just different. Research by the Women's Philanthropy Institute at Indiana University has shown that single women give more than single men; and that in marriage, women socialise their husbands into giving. In addition, women are more likely than men to engage in group giving, with a rising number of women's giving circles setting inspiring examples in their pursuit of joint goals. Female donors are hitting headlines around the globe and millennial women are steering the sector towards further causes and approaches to giving.

The combined growth in women's wealth and their philanthropic engagement is encouraging news. It is also a substantial driver for the future of philanthropy.

*"With the thrust towards giving early in mind, the rise of young philanthropists – and specifically, of millennial women – is particularly encouraging. They engage with a drive for impact and a focus on issues they care about, aiming to make a lasting difference in the world."*

## 2. Engaging early

I have come to believe that a key path towards that future is for wealth owners to give early. Sooner rather than later. In fact, ideally, now.

What I have experienced as an adviser to female philanthropists is that they devote a lot of time to carefully planning their philanthropic journey. Women tend to be risk averse and spend much time deliberating on their values, their vision for change and their giving strategy. This is especially true for owners of larger fortunes and where a charitable foundation or trust holds their wealth. This understandable approach, unfortunately, may lead to frustrations and a long lead time before a first grant is made. Clarity on values and vision is critical; but with the rapidly changing world in which we live, there is also a need for philanthropists to step into action and adjust their giving as they move ahead.

Women's philanthropy is usually fuelled by empathy and executed with a good slice of perfectionism. Care should be taken that giving is not too straining. Philanthropy should lead to a feeling of deep satisfaction and joy by being able to help and do good. Starting early with outright donations, even small ones, allows wealth owners to get involved. Philanthropists can learn from these experiences, step by step, and do good without feeling burdened. This helps them to gain clarity on their future philanthropic journey and the giving structure.

That said, a good way into philanthropy is to do a trial – be it a small donation as a test or a real on-the-ground experience. The vision of one of our female clients was to set up an orphanage in Asia. Given her active lifestyle, we suggested a test run. I knew a philanthropist who had successfully set up a well-known orphanage in Nepal herself, with a clear vision and full dedication. The charity also ran various women's empowerment projects, including a simple guesthouse. We were able to secure a two-week, hands-on volunteering trip for our client to learn, first hand, what it meant to run an orphanage. After what we called this 'immersion trip', our client realised that she would not set up her own organisation. She understood how much time and dedication this would require, and started to focus on research for existing institutions to which she could donate funds, her time and all the knowledge she had gained professionally in Asia throughout her professional career.

With the thrust towards giving early in mind, the rise of young philanthropists – and specifically, of millennial women – is particularly encouraging. They engage with a drive for impact and a focus on issues they care about, aiming to make a lasting difference in the world. Their donations are no longer a matter of legacy funding or grants following the sale of a business. Their philanthropic engagement is no longer just the generous donating or endowing of funds to good causes, promoting the welfare of others; but also about lending a voice, sharing know-how, experience and networks, and building effective, large-scale collaborations.

One of these young role models is Liesel Pritzker Simmons, a Hyatt hotel heiress and one of the co-founders of The Impact, a global membership community of families committed to aligning their assets with their values. Pritzker Simmons also co-founded the Blue Haven Initiative with her husband, Ian Simmons, and developed a reputation for being one of the most driven and passionate individuals in the environmental, social and governance and impact investing communities. The couple's focus is on investing in early-stage businesses aimed at improving quality of life and offering economic opportunities for people in sub-Saharan Africa. "We don't have it all figured out," she told a journalist at worth.com. "We're learning as we go. But we firmly believe that perfect is the enemy of the good ... So if I sit on the sidelines and wait for something to be perfect, it's never going to get there."[6]

For Pritzker Simmons, philanthropy is about more than just passing wealth down through generations; it's about passing along values as well. "I want to be a really responsible steward of these assets," she explains. "I want to be able to say to my kids, 'These are the values that I was raised with. These are the values you were raised with.'"[7]

**3. Engaging collaboratively**

Many women of wealth are seeking to make a real difference through their philanthropy. Often they come across the same challenges and obstacles. There is a desire to share, exchange, collaborate and learn in a 'secure' environment. Many come to the conclusion that collective giving allows them to do just that and, crucially, to increase real impact.

Such giving circles and donor networks come in many forms and shapes. In Switzerland, Atalanti Moquette, a well-known philanthropist based in Geneva, established Giving Women in 2009, which has inspired and empowered hundreds of donors. Under the motto "Empowering women to empower women", the women – not all large donors – have joined to collectively donate towards projects for women in need. The members pool their time, knowledge, professional experience, financial means and ideas in order to be more informed and effective givers.

In the United States, Sondra Shaw-Hardy – philanthropist and co-founder and adjunct professor at the Women's Philanthropy Institute at Indiana University – co-founded Women's Giving Circles International (WGCI) in 2018, in recognition of the power of women to

*"Many women of wealth are seeking to make a real difference through their philanthropy. Often they come across the same challenges and obstacles."*

create change through their philanthropy. WGCI's mission is to grow, nurture and sustain women's collective giving around the world. Through education, giving circles and networks, women join together to become philanthropic leaders, making policy and programme decisions that impact on women and girls at a local level and an international scale. Collectively, they have the power to change and focus on equity, education, healthcare, equality and the environment. Driven by research, WGCI leverages each woman's unique perspective, talent and capacity to ensure a future that is brighter for children, and for being female. "The power of women's philanthropy has changed not only the countries we live in, but changed us as well," states Carmen Stevens, executive director of WGCI. The international platform facilitates circle creation and provides mentorship and educational resources for women all over the globe looking to start and grow their own giving circles. The broad, diverse and inclusive memberships are a critical component to success, as members join forces to serve the needs of women and girls. A key aspect of their work that I like in particular is their concept of democratising philanthropy: giving women, including their younger members, opportunities for joint philanthropy that they may not have individually.

A further high-profile example of a collaborative philanthropic platform is Co-Impact. The non-profit, founded by Olivia Leland in late

2017, focuses on gender equality and is aimed at systemic change. Its members include well-known leaders – men and women – from around the globe. As Co-Impact's website states, "Philanthropy can make significant resources available to support the transformation of underlying systems and redress entrenched discrimination. But too often not enough money is being spent, or funds are spent in ways that do not address systemic barriers – and particularly to the advancement of women and girls." By pooling funds towards long-term systems change to address the root causes of social problems, greater impact can be achieved and learning is accelerated.

Joint learning has also been the focus of a Swiss network for female philanthropists established in Zurich in 2012. I had realised that many philanthropists I was talking with had similar concerns, questions, needs and even frustrations. However, these were not shared and discussed when they would meet at social events and other occasions. This encouraged me to initiate an exclusive space for women philanthropists to come together to exchange ideas, learn from each other and enrich their own giving journeys. The outcome is truly motivating. Members are inspired and energised, and appreciate the valuable connections they make. There is no joint selection of projects or joint funding – it's all about sharing, learning and doing. Some were

*"There is no financial return on being a philanthropist, but there should be an emotional dividend. This can be the joy of seeing supported children grow older and finish school; but it can also entail continuing a powerful philanthropic family legacy."*

able to use and adapt concepts, processes and ideas that other members had implemented in their own philanthropy; while others started to collaborate regionally. There were intense discussions about the importance of values and visions, and whether one should establish a family foundation or grant big sums towards an existing charity. There were presentations on the positive aspects of mission-aligned investments and debates on whether impact investing was an effective approach. All of these open discussions broadened members' views, offered inspiration and enabled them to take better decisions. Working with multi-generational families, I was also intrigued by the potential challenges of 'inheriting philanthropy'. Upon the death of her father, one of our members became the chair of a charity to grant academic scholarships to scientists. At heart, however, she was passionate about helping children in developing countries and had set up her own successful charity in Southern India for children with HIV. How could she manage two such differing approaches to doing good? Would continuing the family philanthropy become a burden; and how would she feel if she did not step in as her family had wished? There is no financial return on being a philanthropist, but there should be an emotional dividend. This can be the joy of seeing supported children grow older and finish school; but it can also entail continuing a powerful philanthropic family legacy.

**4. Engaging strategically**

Whatever objectives one sets, seeing them achieved is among the biggest rewards of philanthropic engagements. Giving strategically by setting goals and evaluating impact is at the core of this. Often used by bigger foundations, strategic giving can help any grant making to be more effective, with contributions being measurable, scalable and sustainable. This requires time and discipline; but in the end, it helps to build a path towards meaningful result.

In our engagement with philanthropists, we typically start with defining the values and vision of the donor, or even an entire family. We have often found this step to be particularly critical for female donors to express their wishes and build confidence to move ahead. Discussing what they can add in terms of the so-called '3 Ts' of philanthropy – time, talent and treasure – is also at the core of setting their space to flourish, inspire and have a lasting impact.

Once donors are clear on the larger purpose of their giving, a strategic plan helps to focus on achieving the agreed goals. The journey is not an easy one. There is so much need, imbalance and injustice on our planet. Many problems just seem too big to solve. And there is a vast amount of non-profits to support. A strategic plan will help to determine the criteria on how to select grantees and how to say no to the many organisations that are excellent, but outside of the scope of one's focus. Whereas there is power in intuition and emotion, it is important to strike a balance with rational decision making. A clear and narrow focus of your grant making helps to funnel limited resources. A portfolio model with a limited number of organisations that share common characteristics – such as a regional focus, a need, an approach or a sector – makes sense. With this model, philanthropists can make larger gifts to fewer organisation over a longer period of time. It also makes it easier, but at the same time more important, to measure the impact of their giving, which will ultimately lead to greater donor satisfaction. Furthermore, it allows philanthropists to take action where organisations are struggling.

A key example of a strategic donor is the Bill and Melinda Gates Foundation. Not only the size of its grants – a total of $53.8 billion in the first 20 years of its existence – but also its goals and long-term approach are highly strategic. In addition, as Mark Honigsbaum writes on the foundation's website: "Their success is built on leverage: specifically, the ability of the Gateses with their smaller but more flexibly deployable pot of money to forge coalitions with large international organisations and governments that can in turn mobilise many more billions of dollars than the Gates Foundation can alone."[8]

In June 2021, the Gates Foundation announced a commitment of over $2 billion to advance gender equality globally over the next five years.[9] The focus is on family planning and health, economic empowerment and accelerating women's leadership. As Melinda French Gates highlights: "The world has been fighting for gender equality for decades, but progress has been slow. Now is the chance to reignite a movement and deliver real change. The beauty of our fight for gender equality is that every human being will gain from it. We must seize this moment to build a better, more equal future."[10]

Having a clear strategy is just as important on a smaller scale. One of the foundations we take care of has been funding an organisation that had been supporting housing and education for children in the slums of Bogota for a number of years. During a long conversation with the organisation's founder, a medical doctor, I realised that she had lost focus and energy. Desperate to make ends meet, the organisation had accepted donations with strings attached, which were not aligned with the strategy; nor did the staff have the skills required. The foundation board decided to pay the allocated funds under the condition that a specialised strategy consultant was hired and paid from the grant. The founder accepted that she and the team needed help and accepted our offer. Today, they are financially stable and following through on their mission of providing quality childcare, offering a safe place to learn and play, complemented by nutritional and psychological support.

*"A portfolio model with a limited number of organisations that share common characteristics – such as a regional focus, a need, an approach or a sector – makes sense."*

Increasingly, those engaged in strategic philanthropy are putting a spotlight on what is probably the most critical ingredient for their impact: trust. In that context, a novel movement known as 'trust-based philanthropy' redefines the relationships between donors and the organisations that rely on their funding, and shifts the onus onto funders to better understand their grantees and their theories of change. Their beliefs are to give multi-year grants and to provide unrestricted funding, as the work of non-profits is long term and unpredictable. This allows for innovation, emergent action and sustainability.

A female philanthropist making headlines along the lines of trust-based philanthropy is MacKenzie Scott. Between mid-2019 and mid-2021 Scott – the ex-wife of Jeff Bezos, in the "process of giving away the majority of her wealth" (at the time of writing over $60 billion) – has granted in excess of $8.6 billion. Her funding is unrestricted, with no strings attached, giving power to the organisations she supports. Much of the funding is going to what Scott calls causes that are generally underfunded and overlooked, including equity, functional democracy and climate change; but there is also a clear focus on supporting women and girls. As a CEO of one of the grantees stated: "Ms. Scott's generosity is quite literally changing the game for women and girls across the globe."[11]

Indeed, much has been written about the belief that the fastest way to end extreme poverty is to invest in girls and women. When girls and women are healthy, safe and educated, they help to transform societies and lift their communities and entire nations out of poverty. At the Maverick Collective – a women's network of strategic philanthropists, each investing $1 million or more over two to three years to create change – a pilot for an innovative solution for girls and women in the developing world is underway. According to co-founder and co-chair Her Royal Highness Crown Princess Mette-Marit of Norway: "The Sustainable Development Goals make a clear call for more advocates, greater innovation, new resources and a sharp focus on improving the health and rights of girls and women ... When everyone contributes what they have to offer, we help lift girls and women everywhere."[12]

**5. Increasing impact**

So, with women on the rise, where is female philanthropy heading?

Silvia Bastante de Unverhau, a philanthropy expert and former global head of philanthropy advisory at UBS, expects women philanthropists to continue to redefine what impactful philanthropy is in the years to come: "From giving more significantly and without restrictions, to engaging in collective giving, practising giving while living, and also giving beyond financial resources, women will fuel these trends and hopefully also influence others for more impactful philanthropy."[13]

As a result, the role of female philanthropy in society will rise – not the glamour of fundraising dinners, but hands-on, intentional and focused giving. In addition, the trend to spend down will increase. As one of my female clients once said: "I want my children to see the world, the beauty and all its imperfections. I want to inspire them to help, but I don't want to hand over the burden to manage and carry the weight of a traditional philanthropic foundation. The young generation today has new ideas – and this is what the world needs."

Indeed, as new forms of philanthropy emerge, female philanthropy is also becoming younger. A growing number of female and male next-gen leaders are increasing the effectiveness of philanthropic impact through both their grant making and their investments. They are engaged and don't shy away from the spotlight of social media. And they are heard. Proud of their heritage, they will not follow in the footsteps of their ancestors, trying to discreetly mould the family's traditional grant making. They are grounded, innovative, strong-minded; and they will do it their way – bigger, faster and louder.

As highlighted by Natasha Müller, a next-gen impact investor and philanthropist: "A new generation of investors is here. We are younger.

We are female. We are principled. And we are determined to find a third way of investing; one that is reflective of values and is meaningful. Women are powerhouses in engaging our networks in causes we champion and believe in, and will only continue to get more creative and infuse new energy into their investing and ways of giving."[14]

Female wealth, power and purpose will be a critical driver of systemic change moving forward. Their philanthropic engagements will be a key catalyst towards an inclusive and sustainable future.

### 6. Additional resources

- Indiana University-Purdue University Indianapolis Lilly Family School of Philanthropy Research, "How and Why Women Give", May 2015 https://philanthropy.iupui.edu/institutes/womens-philanthropy-institute/library/index.html
- RBC Wealth Management, "The new face of wealth and legacy: How women are redefining wealth, giving and legacy planning", 2018 www.rbcwealthmanagement.com/us/en/research-insights/the-new-face-of-wealth-and-legacy-how-women-are-redefining-wealth-giving-and-legacy-planning/detail/

Further links to Giving Circles and other philanthropic initiatives:

- Women's Giving Circles International – www.wgci.online
- Co-Impact – www.co-impact.org
- Giving Women – https://givingwomen.ch
- Maverick Collective – https://maverickcollective.org
- The Trust-Based Philanthropy Project – https://trustbasedphilanthropy.org

### Notes

1 Boston Consulting Group (BCG), *Managing the Next Decade of Women's Wealth*, 9 April 2020, www.bcg.com/publications/2020/managing-next-decade-women-wealth.
2 UBS, *Women's Wealth 2030: Parity, Power and Purpose*, 8 March 2021, www.ubs.com/global/en/wealth-management/women/2021/women-wealth-parity-power-purpose.html.
3 Charities Aid Foundation, *The Crucial, Growing Role of Women in Philanthropy*, 2021, www.cafonline.org/my-personal-giving/philanthropy-change-makers/women-in-philanthropy.
4 McKinsey, *Women as the next wave of growth in US wealth management*, 29 July 2020, www.mckinsey.com/industries/financial-services/our-insights/women-as-the-next-wave-of-growth-in-us-wealth-management.
5 BGC (n 1).
6 "Liesel Pritzker Simmons' Family Values", *Worth*, www.worth.com/liesel-pritzker-simmons-family-values/.
7 *Ibid.*
8 The Bill and Melinda Gates Foundation, "Our Story", www.gatesfoundation.org/about/our-story; "How do you solve a problem like Malaria", 11 November 2021, www.gatesfoundation.org/ideas/articles/advances-and-challenges-in-solving-global-malaria.
9 CNBC, "Gates Foundation commits $2.1 billion over the next five years to gender equality", 30 June 2021, www.cnbc.com/2021/06/30/gates-foundation-commits-2point1-billion-to-gender-equality-over-next-5-years.html.

10 This Day, "Advancing Gender Equality Globally", 19 July 2021 www.thisdaylive.com/index.php/2021/07/19/advancing-gender-equality-globally/.
11 CNN Business, "MacKenzie Scott, formerly Bezos, says she has given away $1.7 billion of her wealth so far", 28 July 2020, https://edition.cnn.com/2020/07/28/tech/mackenzie-scott-bezos-donation/index.html.
12 Maverick Collective, https://maverickcollective.org.
13 Quote given to author.
14 Quote given to author.

# IX. Family philanthropy and cultural purposes

**Christian von Oertzen**
**Tanja Schienke-Ohletz**
Flick Gocke Schaumburg Partnerschaft mbB

## 1. Introduction

While the term 'philanthropy' has a generally understood meaning, most tax laws use the word to describe organisations that are tax exempt due to their charitable purposes. Most philanthropic organisations are organised and operated for specific purposes, which may qualify for tax-exempt status according to the applicable tax law. Stated purposes include charitable, religious, scientific, literary and educational purposes; prevention of cruelty to animals; development cooperation; and sports. However, another very important purpose is art and culture or the protection of monuments.

There are many ways in which a family can pursue cultural philanthropic purposes. For example, they could found a charitable organisation or donate funds to existing charitable organisations that themselves pursue cultural purposes. It is also possible to gift art or monuments or art collections to other persons, and to benefit from a tax privilege or a tax exemption under certain conditions.

However, family philanthropy is not about tax planning. It is about family legacy planning by involving the family, developing values which help family members to understand each other as individuals and encourage them take care of each other. It is not about managing a portfolio's value, but rather about cultivating and preserving a family identity.

**2. Cultural purposes**

The cultural purposes of art and culture are usually defined in tax laws as charitable purposes and are tax exempt. The pursuit of art and culture usually includes the preservation of cultural values through the efforts of cultural institutions such as theatres and museums, and cultural events such as concerts and art exhibitions. It also includes painting and the cinematic arts. The purpose of art and culture is not reduced to certain art forms; rather, art and culture are free creative actions in which an artist expresses his or her impressions and experiences. Video art, for example, also qualifies as art and culture. Some charitable organisations grant awards for the artworks of younger artists or scholarships for young artists to develop their talents.

**3. Initial questions**

If a family is keen to support arts and culture, they should first consider how and what kind of cultural purposes they want to foster – for example, a museum or a certain art style. Are there defined family values to consider – for example, should a family art collection be made available to the general public or should scientific research be undertaken? Which resources could the family use? Should the local theatre receive cash donations? Should the family be involved in running the cultural organisation? Who in the family will be involved in the philanthropic giving and who will have decision-making power? Should a family art collection be expanded over the generations or should it be preserved as it was first established?

A family adviser would be wise to determine why the family wants to pursue cultural purposes and who in the family is the key driver for doing so. It is also very important to determine whether the next generation has a passion for pursuing cultural purposes or whether it is only the desire of the older generation; and whether the patriarch or matriarch wishes to build a monument to himself or herself, and the planning is more about protecting the art collection against future heirs rather than expanding it further after the collector has passed on. Older generations may impose restrictions and younger generations may have different interests and ideas in terms of philanthropy. Depending on the answers, it may be difficult to choose the ideal structure for the family philanthropy from the various models available.

Figure 1 sets out some important questions that a family adviser can raise in order to find out more about the family's interests and determine which philanthropic planning model fits best.

**Figure 1. Decision making for families**

Identify as a family a common culture purpose

Are there existing family values that should be maintained?

Own charity or charitable giving?

Which resources can be used – art collection or funds?

Who will have decision-making power in the family?

Who will be responsible in the next generation?

## 4. Structural forms for cultural purposes

### 4.1 Founding the family's 'own' charity

One possible structure for supporting cultural purposes is to establish the family's own charity in the form of a foundation or, in the Anglo-American world, in the form of a trust, which runs its own family museum. This structure requires the greatest involvement of the family. The establishment of a foundation may also mean that the family must transfer its art collection or at least substantial amounts of cash to the foundation; and this transfer cannot usually be easily revoked. Such a transfer should be carefully considered within the family, as the foundation will be the new owner of the art collection or substantial other assets. If the art collection will be exhibited in the family's own private museum, the museum will be staffed with family wealth and at least one of the family members in every generation will oversee the operations.

This organisational form is not chosen very often. One example is the Frieder Burda Museum in Baden-Baden. Mr Burda donated his outstanding modern art collection to a charity he created and also built the museum. Family members continue to be members of the supervisory board. Under their stewardship – and with the help of external advisers, art historians and exhibition planners – the museum continues to develop.

Another famous example of a testamentary bequest to a foundation is the Städel Museum in Frankfurt. In this case, banker Mr Städel – who had a collection of artworks by important 18th century Dutch painters – stated in his last will that the art collection should be made available to the public, and that a foundation should be established after his death for this purpose. After a long dispute with his legal heirs, who tried to challenge the will, a foundation was established. The German Civil Code states explicitly that a foundation can be established upon death and can have retroactive effect even if formal steps towards the establishment are necessary after the founder's death. This example shows that the idea of philanthropy has been important to art collectors for centuries. However, in order to avoid any disputes, it is recommended to discuss the idea with the family *inter vivos.*

**4.2 Corporate governance in a foundation**

Once a foundation has been established, it should be determined how decisions will be made. Will this be by consensus or majority? Would it be useful to have family members on the management board or supervisory board, or instead to delegate these responsibilities to external third parties? Are staff needed and if so, what powers should they have? Corporate governance is an important issue when a family is establishing its own foundation. Foundations in German law usually have one management board, but they can also choose to have a supervisory board that controls the management's decisions. Often, the owner of the art collection is both the founder and a member of the management board of the foundation. Careful thought should be given to whether family members are interested in continuing the family tradition and being active members of the management board and assuming responsibility for the projects of the foundation. One solution may be to establish a supervisory board that controls the

*"Careful thought should be given to whether family members are interested in continuing the family tradition and being active members of the management board and assuming responsibility for the projects of the foundation."*

management board, and to provide in the statutes of the foundation that a majority of the members of the supervisory board will be family members (see Figure 2). Upon the founder's death, the supervisory board nominates and recalls the members of the management and can exercise influence over essential decisions.

**Figure 2. Corporate government structure where the family has a majority on the supervisory board**

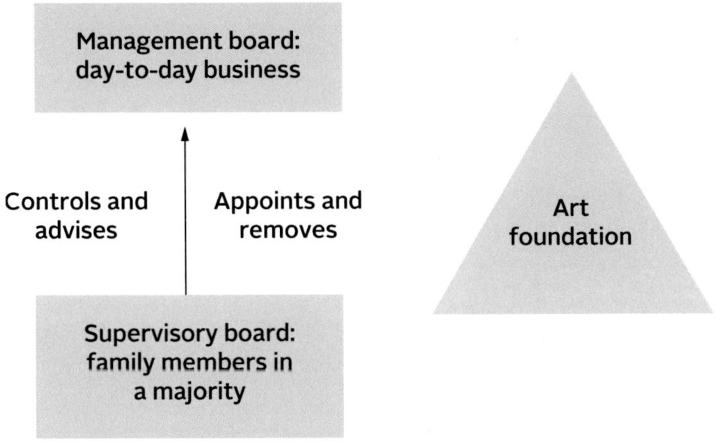


Alternatively, it may be that the founder is a member of the management board and is responsible for the foundation's day-to-day business. It may not be entirely clear whether the next generation will be willing to play an active role in the business of the foundation and whether they have the skills and expertise to do so. In this case, the corporate governance must be considered carefully. It is generally recommended that a foundation have not only a management board, but also a supervisory board, to ensure a separation of powers.

In the statues of the foundation, two scenarios may be taken into account. First, it may be that one day a family member may develop an interest in running the foundation. If there is a supervisory board comprised of external third parties with various interests, there is a risk that they may be able to remove the family member as manager; or that the focus of the foundation's activities may shift to something that has nothing to do with the founder's original idea. To avoid this happening, the statutes should provide that, for example, a family member as manager of the foundation has certain special privileges – for example, the right to remain in his or her position for life without risk of removal. In this case, the supervisory board has only restricted powers to control the management board and has more of a representative function. However, if there is no family member who intends to engage in the foundation, the founder should specify in the statutes of the foundation who will be his or her successors, or who will appoint his or her successors if he or she can no longer exercise his or her position. A scenario where the foundation's management can appoint the future manager of the foundation and it could thus fall out of the family's control should be avoided. The future manager should be someone whom the founder trusts or someone with special expertise in the relevant field of art. Otherwise, there is a risk that the family may lose its influence and the foundation will be governed by persons outside the family. In this case, there is a risk that the family's values and ideas will no longer be represented in the foundation.

**Figure 3. Example corporate government structure where the family operates the management board**

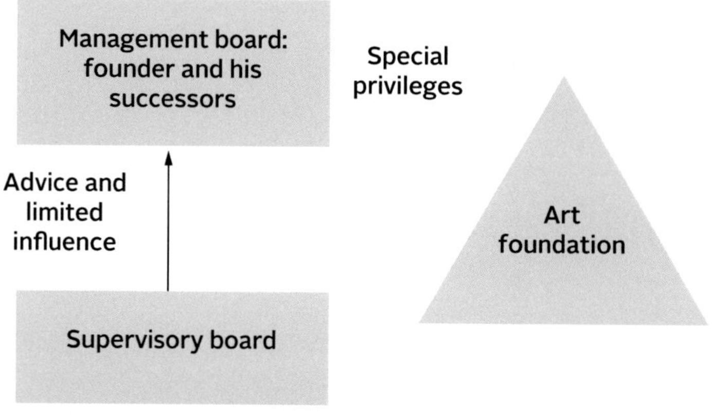


### 5. Cooperation agreements

Less far reaching than a separate family charity is a cooperation agreement with a private or public art museum, under which all or some of the art collection may be sent on loan to the museum. The loan agreement will determine in particular whether some parts of the art collection will be shown as a permanent exhibition or in special exhibitions; and whether the family will make annual cash donations. The loan term is usually more than a decade – sometimes for more than 30 years; and sometimes the loan agreement provides for the donation of a piece of art from the collection to the museum. Also, if the family wants to sell a piece from the collection, the museum will often have a pre-emptive right to buy.

The negotiations on the loan agreement between the private collector and the public museum may be delicate. On the one hand, any museum would be happy to find a private collector who is willing to loan his or her art collection to it. On the other hand, a public museum must give primacy to the interests of the public; and any strong board of trustees of a museum will wish to have the freedom to develop the museum further or to change parts of a permanent collection as it wishes, and will not want to become merely the extended arm of a private collector. Every museum will wish to remain independent.

An example from Germany that illustrates this delicate relationship is the story of Hermann Josef Abs and the Städel Museum in Frankfurt. Hermann Josef Abs was a very influential private banker in West Germany and the owner of a very large 18th century art collection. He was also one of the administrators of the Städel Museum and was well known for his fundraising activities for the museum. Later on in life, he started trying to influence who would become future directors of the museum. Reportedly, he did so by threatening to change his will so that the art collection would not pass to the museum on his death if certain people were not promoted or certain art movements were not championed. When he passed away, he left an incomplete will which was void and his art collection never passed to the museum.

A private collector should understand that a public museum is of general interest both to other collectors and to the public, and should be able to develop its own profile over the generations. Thus, for some private collectors a loan agreement with a museum may be of interest instead. This allows the collector to remain the owner of the artworks, while dedicating the artworks to the public temporarily.

### 5.1 Terms of a loan agreement

The following issues should be considered when negotiating a loan agreement:

- Should the duration of the loan be fixed or flexible?
- Should any special reasons for termination be specified?
- Which parts of the art collection will be shown to the public, which artworks will be included and in what context?
- Can the artworks be published in a special catalogue or another medium? Can the museum lend them to other museums or use them for special exhibitions?
- What will it cost to insure the art collection/artworks? Will the insurance be covered by the museum?
- Who is responsible for transporting the artworks and how will they be preserved?
- Under what conditions will the artworks be stored (eg, humidity, temperature, brightness)?
- Are conservatory works planned during the loan period and who will manage and pay for them?

## 6. 'Friends of' organisations

Another way to foster art in collaboration with a museum is through the creation of a 'friends of' organisation, involving the family in fundraising activities with the museum. The budgets of 'friends of' organisations can be used to redecorate a room in the museum, finance the studies of an art historian or help to buy the 'missing link' in an art collection.

A 'friends of' organisation can also be affiliated with the art department in a local university, providing scholarships or ateliers for young artists. For example, the *Städel Schule* in Frankfurst is a college for fine arts established in 1817. Initially, Mr Städel's art collection was used to provide show pieces for art classes. Today, the museum and the school are separate from each other. The *Städel Schule* is financed by the city and the state, but a foundation and a 'friends of' organisation also exist that offer scholarships for young artists, provide working materials for students and fund trips to cities such as Rome and Florence. Over the generations, Frankfurt families have assumed roles and responsibilities in the organisation as part of their commitment to contribute to local society.

'Friends of' organisations allow family members to conduct fundraising activities, but there is no further active philanthropic engagement. This can be advantageous if family members are interested in philanthropic engagement, but do not have the time to develop their own projects and ideas.

## 7. Intergenerational involvement of a family

### 7.1 Staying in touch

A very delicate but also very important question is how the next generation of a family will continue their involvement in a charity or 'friends of' organisation established by previous generations. This question is difficult to answer, especially when family members no longer live in their city of origin.

One idea in this situation is to host a family meeting every two or three years in the city of origin. Social media also makes it easy to stay in contact with a charity which was formed by the family matriarch or patriarch.

The older generation should also describe their engagement as part of their lifestyle and part of the family history, and as a positive experience. Philanthropic engagement allows the older generation to share family history, values and principles with the next generation. Family philanthropy can also enable different family members to stay in touch, especially when family members are spread all over the world. It is a great opportunity to foster meaningful relationships across the generations.

### 7.2 On-boarding the younger generation

The younger generation should be involved in decision making as soon as possible. But what happens if the patriarch or matriarch is interested in impressionism, while the younger generation is more interested in contemporary art or video art? The patriarch or

*"A very delicate but also very important question is how the next generation of a family will continue their involvement in a charity or 'friends of' organisation established by previous generations. This question is difficult to answer, especially when family members no longer live in their city of origin."*

matriarch should enter into discussions with the next generation and hear their ideas and how they intend to continue the family's philanthropic ideas, even if they have different ideas. The older generation should allow the next generation to challenge existing systems and suggest new approaches. Otherwise, there is a risk that the younger generation will lose its motivation.

It is also recommended to include younger family members on the management board or supervisory board of a family foundation, so that they learn how to work in philanthropy and participate in such organisations. If the family has entered into a cooperation agreement with a museum, the younger generation should participate in negotiations and have an influence on contractual issues. For the younger generation, philanthropic engagement helps to further their professional and personal development as they learn about the challenges of adult life.

## 8. Conclusions

### 8.1 Culture purpose as common identity

The family should identify certain values and decide which cultural purposes they wish to foster – for example, a certain art style or a museum. Cultural purposes are varied and can change over the course of generations.

### 8.2 Legal form

It should be considered which legal form best suits the family's interest in philanthropic engagement – for example, whether they wish to participate actively in an organisation or just cooperate or fund raise.

### 8.3 Charity

By setting up their own charity, a family can ensure continuity of their philanthropic activities and connect their name with a certain art collection or museum. The corporate governance of a foundation is very important. The founder must consider carefully how he or she can involve the younger generation in the foundation. He or she must also decide whether the family will be represented on the managing board and help to run the day-to-day business of the foundation; or whether they will be represented on the supervisory board and control the board of trustees. He or she must also look out for a successor who will be able to make decisions for the next generation. An appropriate and sophisticated corporate government structure is thus necessary. The founder should take the time to develop and discuss these proposals in the family. The founder should also determine how family members will engage in this structure and how their influence can be maintained in order to ensure that the charitable purpose of the foundation continues.

*"The founder should take the time to develop and discuss these proposals in the family. The founder should also determine how family members will engage in this structure and how their influence can be maintained in order to ensure that the charitable purpose of the foundation continues."*

### 8.4 Cooperation agreement

A cooperation agreement with a museum to lend it an art collection is another option. However, negotiations over loan agreements between private collectors and public museums are often challenging. The private collector must ensure not only that his or her interests are safeguarded in the loan agreement, but also that the museum can remain neutral and is not reduced to a mere showroom of the private collector. These interests must be balanced out in the relationship and in the agreement.

### 8.5 'Friends of' organisation

Another way to engage is through a so-called 'friends of' organisation, which undertakes fundraising activities for a specific museum. This enables the family to develop contacts and learn how to fundraise for cultural purposes.

### 8.6 Intergenerational challenges

It is possible that many family members may live in other countries, which presents a further challenge. Despite their geographical location, they should be encouraged to develop a shared idea of philanthropic activity – for example, by visiting a museum or their own charity or art collection. The younger generation should also have a voice in discussions about the future of the family's philanthropic activities, as otherwise they will be unable to continue this valuable work. The older generation must thus liaise with the younger generation to find a compromise on all ideas. The younger generation should also be on-boarded in the charity or in other philanthropic activities, to prepare them to take over important roles in the future.

*"Our legacy – both positive and negative – is the degree to which we shine light or create darkness around us, shaping an environment for others to thrive or falter. We do this on a moment-by-moment basis. The only moment we have is the present moment."*

# X. A thoughtful legacy

**Diana Chambers**
The Chambers Group Sàrl

*You cannot get through a single day without having an impact on the world around you. What you do makes a difference, and you have to decide what kind of difference you want to make.*
Jane Goodall

**1. Introduction**

"Our legacy – both positive and negative – is the degree to which we shine light or create darkness around us, shaping an environment for others to thrive or falter. We do this on a moment-by-moment basis. The only moment we have is the present moment."[1]

Those of us with more financial resources than we need for our wellbeing have a tremendous opportunity to have an outsized impact on our communities and societies. As a Family Wealth Mentor™ and philanthropic adviser for the last 20 years, I propose that the opportunity to give generously from our resources is the ultimate luxury. I have seen how much joy thoughtful, strategic gifts bring to the giver. I support my clients in finding the optimal ways to express their generosity – whether through an outright gift or investing for social impact – because we all want to know that our giving has made a positive difference.

Society is at a catalytic moment. Many of our old systems are visibly fraying at their edges. #MeToo and Black Lives Matter illustrate the gross inadequacies of our current approaches. Gender and racial norms are being questioned and required to change. Our planet is hurtling at breakneck speed towards a situation where living conditions are becoming intolerable for large swathes of the world's population. The climate is becoming increasingly inhospitable: heatstroke is making it impossible for many workers to continue with their outdoor trades and activities; climate migrants are seeking safe places to call home; farmers are finding it impossible to grow their crops because of drought; and so much more.

I encourage a societal and global perspective on legacy, determining what the world needs most at this critical juncture in history and how we can impact positively the systems that shape our lives. You may not have incorporated this view in your philanthropy to date, but it is compatible with professional guidance and may enrich your legacy journey.

Shaping our legacy is simple and yet paradoxically complex. If you have delved deep into the root causes of a societal challenge, you will know that it is not easy to discern how best to make a positive impact. We hear stories of well-intentioned donors who do not adequately understand the culture in which they are operating and so cause

*"The climate is becoming increasingly inhospitable: heatstroke is making it impossible for many workers to continue with their outdoor trades and activities; climate migrants are seeking safe places to call home; farmers are finding it impossible to grow their crops because of drought; and so much more."*

unintended harm. For example, community social structures may be negatively disrupted by the desire to provide clean water to rural villages. Or the introduction of technology that cannot be simply and effectively maintained can leave local infrastructure worse off than it was before the intervention. And we know that change is inevitable and may reveal new and better ways than we have adopted so far to approach the issue that concerns us. Navigating these complexities requires us to maintain our curiosity and see ourselves not as experts, but as students.

There is another paradox embedded in the shaping of legacy: our legacy is both intimately about us, and not about us. Aldous Huxley put it beautifully:

> *We have to learn, so to speak, to get out of our own light, because with our personal self – this idolatrously worshiped self – we are continually standing in the light of this wider self – this not-self, if you like – which is associated with us and which this standing in the light prevents. We eclipse the illumination from within. And in all the activities of life, from the simplest physical activities to the highest intellectual and spiritual activities, our whole effort must be to get out of our own light.*[2]

In considering a societal perspective on legacy, I offer the following themes for reflection:

- what it means to be philanthropic;
- appreciating your legacy to date;
- considering when to shape your legacy;
- including in your legacy what the world needs now; and
- the impact of your legacy on your descendants.

**2. What it means to be philanthropic**

In financial circles, 'legacy' is often synonymous with the monetary gifts we make during our lives and those we leave for distribution at our deaths, or through the foundations or giving vehicles we have established. But our philanthropic legacy is this and much more, reflecting the generosity of our spirit and the multiple ways in which that might be expressed, as exemplified by Jane Goodall. She has dedicated her life to animal welfare and conservation. She was a trailblazer in the field of primatology and is renowned for her work with chimpanzees. When writing about her for *Time* magazine in 2019, when she was named one of the 100 most influential people in the world, Leonardo DiCaprio said: "Anyone who has heard her speak, or heard her story, has been mesmerized by her life's work and moved by her philanthropic legacy."[3]

Jane Goodall is known for her leadership, tireless activism and inspiration for many initiatives on behalf of animal rights and environmental causes. She has created this legacy by giving of herself to these causes throughout her long life, and she continues to shape her legacy day by day.

Not all of us have the reach of Jane Goodall. Take Laura, for example. She works four days a week as a cook in the health clinic I attend. One day, she told me: "I just love to feed people." And every time she packs me a meal to take home, I find she has included an extra treat; the last time it was an unexpected slice of delicious banana bread. In her spare time, she volunteers regularly at her local zoo. Laura does not have the ability to make significant financial gifts, but she has a generous spirit and casts light around her.

Laura and Jane Goodall are both philanthropic in the true meaning of the word, which is expressing their 'love of humanity'. Their philanthropy – expressions of their generosity and love – includes not only their financial gifts, but also their volunteering, activism and ways of opening their social networks to encourage support for the causes to which they are committed. And each time they express themselves in this way, they lead. Philanthropy at its best uses all available resources for maximum positive effect – all are 'mission-critical'.

We do not have to be publicly acclaimed giants to leave a remarkable legacy; each one of us influences our environment and the people around us. We can be philanthropic, generous and significant every day of our lives through the quality of our relationships and how we connect with everyone with whom we come into contact.

As you reflect on your unique contributions, consider these questions:

- What are your personal attributes?
- How have you been prepared to lead?
- What multiplicity of resources do you have at your disposal?

**3. What is your legacy to date?**

Every single day, our actions create our legacy. By assessing what you have created to date, I hope you will identify many ways in which you have already left a positive and powerful legacy – that your life has counted in significant ways.

I invite you to slow down and take time to reflect on these questions:[4]

- Whom did you include in your 'family'? (Nuclear, community, national, global?)
- What did you do for others?

*"We do not have to be publicly acclaimed giants to leave a remarkable legacy; each one of us influences our environment and the people around us. We can be philanthropic, generous and significant every day of our lives through the quality of our relationships and how we connect with everyone with whom we come into contact."*

- Were you available?
- Were you generous?
- Did you listen well?
- Did you love well?
- Did you shine light or cast darkness around you?

In whatever ways you have acted in these areas to date, you can start consciously to shape your legacy today with these questions to guide you.

**4. When to shape your legacy**
"From success to significance" was a phrase I often heard in the early 2000s. It was used to capture the transition that people made, typically in their 50s, as they had attained substantial financial success and were then poised to launch their philanthropic activities. But it misses the point that we shape our legacy every day of our lives. My invitation to you is consciously to shape your legacy now, whatever your age. You can be significant every day of your life, so why postpone your financial philanthropic expression until some date in the future when you think you will have time to do your gifting effectively?

Jonas Salk, the pioneering scientist who developed the first effective and safe polio vaccine, said: "Our greatest responsibility is to be good ancestors."[5] In his 1992 paper, he asked: "Will we have the wisdom to perceive the long as well as short-term advantages in the choices we make so as to enhance the quality of our own lives and of the generations to follow? ... It is relevant and even part of wisdom to ask not only are we being good citizens of the world today, but are we being good ancestors."[6]

Roman Krznaric's book *The Good Ancestor* was published early in 2021. On hearing him interviewed,[7] I appreciated how he highlighted our obsession with the present – "the tyranny of the now" – as many of us have "colonized the future". He invites us to get our existence in context and "stretch our imaginations beyond the present tense".

To be a good ancestor means to shed light around you and to light the path ahead for your descendants. A woman in her 20s – an inheritor from a powerful, wealthy family – once asked me how she was meant to relate to her wealth knowing that her ancestors had destroyed many human lives to build their fortune. The money she inherited cast a shadow over her and she was struggling to find a redemptive way forward.

In more recent years, Salk's wisdom has been shaped into the phrase "Be a good ancestor now", emphasising that every moment counts. When I first heard this phrase, seven years ago, I was so taken with it

*"Our societal status quo is untenable – evidenced by the visible impacts of systemic racism, gender inequality and climate change – regardless of what one believes to be the cause."*

that I had it printed on mugs that I gifted to clients to give them a ready reminder about our role in the world and how to think about ourselves, our behaviour and what we contribute.

Reflection questions:

- In what ways do you shine light or cast darkness around and ahead of you?
- What avenues for generosity and love are most relevant for you today?

**5. What will be your future legacy?**
Donors want to know that their gifts are purposeful. A standard approach is to encourage an individual or family to assess their values and then express them in their personal interest areas, or through their 'passion projects'. This is a great way to get immediate engagement, maintain motivation and satisfy the donor. But let me pose some broader questions:

- Is this what the world needs most right now?
- What does the world need today to be sustainable and humane for your descendants and others?

Our societal status quo is untenable – evidenced by the visible impacts of systemic racism, gender inequality and climate change – regardless of what one believes to be the cause. The fallout will affect us all, however insulated we might feel we are from the most severe effects. The global experience of the COVID-19 pandemic is a perfect example of how interconnected we are and how we need to care for the whole of humanity for any one of us to thrive.

I invite my clients to reflect on their roles as philanthropists in light of the tectonic shifts we are witnessing. Our work as positive change agents is to develop the wisdom and take the time necessary to discern the undercurrents of society and to support the new to emerge as painlessly and creatively as possible. As Aldous Huxley said, we need to get out of our own light and allow the light of the wider self to shine. This is much easier said than done.

There is no right way to assess and rank different societal needs that you may choose to address through your philanthropy. For example, it is impossible to say whether it is more important to feed someone who is hungry than to provide rape crisis counselling for survivors of abuse. We can only answer "Yes!" to both.

Wherever there is pain and suffering, there is a role for change agents. If your philanthropic commitment is local and directed to the communities that have been the source of your wealth, I encourage you to determine how to support systems change at the local level and to understand how the grants you are making are part of constructively turning the tide to change underlying structures to be healthier for all concerned. Sherry Turkle, professor of the social studies of science and technology at Massachusetts Institute of Technology, has made it her work to look under the surface of the familiar by questioning our assumptions and looking for hidden truths. In an interview with the Greater Good Science Center,[8] she said: "I became a kind of anthropologist, developing a habit of taking an outsider's view. Most importantly, when I came into any new situation, the question always in the back of my mind was, *What else is happening here? I see what's happening on the surface, but what is in the depths?"* She went on to say that changing a system requires that we "make the familiar unfamiliar. It's helps to talk to other people and to ask, *What's wrong with this picture?"*

Here are four tips as you consider your role in systems change.

First, systems change is intensely demanding work, requiring fundamental shifts in world views. If your commitment as a philanthropist is not overtly focused on systems change, then as a client of mine said: "At least we must try not to work against any positive systemic change." This philanthropist identified three lenses through which consciously to assess all potential grants to ensure that, at the very least, they do no harm:

- systemic racism;
- the wellbeing of women and girls; and
- environmental health.

Second, systems change requires a sophisticated donor who does not need to be encouraged on a regular basis by surface wins. Hopefully, we will live long enough to see the fruits of our commitment; but the real issue is staying faithful to the work while changing course when we get new insights into the best path forwards.

Third, changing a system cannot be done alone. It requires dedicated partners. While as philanthropists we contribute financial resources and more, we must recognise the vital contributions of other participants – visionaries, activists, community leaders, researchers, artists, the media and many others – without whom progress would stall. Each one is contributing what they can bring to the table. Your partners "give you an opportunity to express your passion and concerns for the world, and you give them much-needed financial support. It's a two-way street; you enhance each other".[9]

*"While as philanthropists we contribute financial resources and more, we must recognise the vital contributions of other participants – visionaries, activists, community leaders, researchers, artists, the media and many others – without whom progress would stall."*

Fourth, I am convinced that the underlying cause of the broken structures and relationships in our world is trauma. Trauma is the inner response in the body and nervous system of a person who goes through an overwhelming situation. Trauma creates disconnection within ourselves and separation from others. If we were to feel connected, as opposed to separate, we would be unable to behave as we do – injuring others and destroying the planet on which we depend. While the field of trauma research has evolved greatly over the last 30 years, there has been a recent explosion of interest in the study of trauma as it has found its way into popular thinking. Oprah Winfrey helped to raise awareness of the impact of trauma in her work on education. In 2018, in a CBS News interview, she said: "And really the question that we should be asking is not 'What's wrong with that child?' but 'What happened to that child?'"[10]

At the very least I believe that all philanthropy should be trauma informed and, progressively, trauma transformational as a building block to address society's challenges and as an essential foundation for systemic change. See the appendix below for some resources in this field.

Reflection questions:

- What is your dream for society?
- What is standing in the way of it coming into being?

- What systems change would you like to embed in your philanthropy?
- Who is working in that area?
- How can you together make change happen?

**6. What will your descendants say about you?**
Finally, an issue that is important for many philanthropists: will future generations want to topple a proverbial statue of you or will they recognise that they are "standing on the shoulders of giants"?[11] Will they be proud to claim their heritage from you or will they do their best to disguise their ancestry?

Our heritage typically weaves together multiple mixed threads. As children, we can be tremendously grateful for and proud of our ancestors' values, qualities and actions. We can admire their resilience in times of difficulty; their devotion to their families; their creativity, ingenuity and entrepreneurialism. At the same time, we recognise that our inheritance might have included fear, greed, violence and more. All these threads subsequently play out in our lives and the lives of our children.

As parents, one of our greatest concerns is typically to ensure that our children embody the values we hold dear and become upstanding

*"Including our children in our philanthropy is a great way to help them to understand why we give of ourselves and our wealth and how we choose to express our values."*

contributors to society. Yet we sometimes confuse expression of our core values with the core values themselves. For example, we might hold the value of loyalty which one generation may express in relation to immediate family and the right to life, while another might express loyalty to humanity at large and so to support for refugee populations. While seemingly very different interests, with family members potentially experiencing little common ground, it is helpful to remember that these two causes emerged from the same core value. And as society evolves, the ways in which we express our core values may also evolve.

Including our children in our philanthropy is a great way to help them to understand why we give of ourselves and our wealth and how we choose to express our values. I have been fortunate to work with several families as they embarked on or reviewed their philanthropy, assessing its impact both externally and within the family.

I was recently privileged to consult with a family where the father and his three children, aged in their 30s, were deciding on the structure for their new philanthropic initiatives. Their mother had died when the children were teenagers, yet she was present at the table in spirit. As the children shared stories of what had shaped them, I heard about volunteer activities they participated in with their mother and causes she held dear to her heart and about which she educated them. After completing the initial work to identify their philanthropic direction, one of the children summarised what was clear to everyone in the room: "Mum would have been pleased with our decisions!" In this family, there was a profound and positive influence from both parents on their children, and each generation was proud of the other. Their future shared philanthropy will be one way in which the family's legacy will be consciously expressed.

Reflection questions:

- What would you like your descendants to say about you?
- What actions can you take now to create that scenario?

**7. Conclusion**
I have raised a lot of questions. Asking the right questions and taking time to reflect on them are more important than having all the answers. My hope is that you will slow down in your busy life, sit patiently with these questions and discover their answers as they are revealed to you.

If you engage in this adventure with a spirit of curiosity and are willing to change your mind when the new is revealed, you will be an amazing conduit for a light-filled future.

*"If you engage in this adventure with a spirit of curiosity and are willing to change your mind when the new is revealed, you will be an amazing conduit for a light-filled future."*

**Annex: Resources for understanding the impact of trauma on individuals and society**

Research indicates that we may enter this world coded with the experiences of our ancestors, a number of which were traumatising to them. Yet the influence of trauma in society is so broad and diffuse that it is not questioned, but rather is accepted as normal. It is not normal. The inheritance of ancestral trauma suggests that part of our work is to grow in our own awareness, so we can stop passing to our children any inherited limiting traumas. I recommend the work of several teachers in this field, including:

- Thomas Hübl, *Healing Collective Trauma* (Sounds True, 2020);
- Bessel van der Kolk, *The Body Keeps the Score* (Penguin Books, 2015); and
- Gabor Maté, *The Wisdom of Trauma* (Science and Nonduality, 2021).

**Notes**

1 Diana Chambers, *True Wealth: Letters on Money, Life, and Love* (Altitude Press, 2016).
2 Aldous Huxley, "The Divine Within: Selected Writings on Enlightenment" (HarperPerennial Modern Classics, 1992).
3 Leonardo DiCaprio, "Jane Goodall", *Time* magazine (April 2019), https://time.com/collection/100-most-influential-people-2019/5567774/jane-goodall/.
4 Chambers (n 1).
5 Jonas Salk, as quoted in Liam Fahey and Robert Randall, *Learning from the Future: Competitive Foresight Scenarios* (John Wiley & Sons, Inc, 1998), p332.

6 Jonas Salk "Are We Being Good Ancestors?" *World Affairs: The Journal of International Issues* Vol 1, No 2 (Kapur Surya Foundation 1992), pp16–18.
7 Roman Krznaric, interview with Humanity Rising, Ubiquity University, 18 June 2021.
8 Sherry Turkle, interviewed by Jill Suttie, "Why It's Important to Look Beyond the Surface of Things" Greater Good Science Center, *Greater Good Magazine*, 9 June 2021.
9 Chambers (n 1).
10 Oprah Winfrey explores the impact of childhood trauma on educational accomplishment for *60 Minutes*, CBS News, 6 March 2018.
11 Attributed to Priscian, Bernard of Chartres, and Isaac Newton, who in 1675 said, "If I have seen further it is by standing on the shoulders of Giants."

# About the authors

**Kecia Barkawi**
CEO, founding partner and president of the board, VALUEworks
kecia@valueworks.ch

In 2004, Kecia Barkawi founded VALUEworks, a multi-family office based in Zurich, Switzerland, with the goal to empower families to manage their wealth in a meaningful way, and to nurture a responsible next generation. Today she advises her clients on family governance, philanthropy, estate planning and overall wealth structuring, and coaches female and next-gen clients on how to cope with wealth-related challenges. Kecia serves on a number of boards – foundations, companies and industry bodies – and is a frequent speaker at international conferences.

Kecia worked for Baker McKenzie and GAM, before joining PwC Zurich's private client department as a vice president. She spearheaded the creation of the Swiss Association of Trust Companies, co-founded the Zurich Roundtable of Philanthropy and later initiated the Swiss Women + Philanthropy network.

In 2021 Kecia was awarded for her "Outstanding Contribution to Wealth Management Thought Leadership" and recognised as a "Leading Individual" at *WealthBriefing*'s Swiss Awards; and was named "Top 20 Family Office Adviser" by *Citywealth* in London. Kecia holds a master's in law from the University of Zurich and an MBA from Heriot-Watt University in Edinburgh.

**Donzelina Barroso**
Director of global philanthropy, Rockefeller Philanthropy Advisors
dbarroso@rockpa.org

Donzelina ('Donzie') Barroso serves as director of global philanthropy at Rockefeller Philanthropy Advisors (RPA), working with its major individual, family, corporate and institutional donors from across the globe to implement their philanthropic strategies. In 2017, Donzie launched RPA's first international office, in London. She has two decades of experience in international grant making and project management, including work in education, the arts, health and human services, community development and the Sustainable Development Goals and environmental issues. Donzie has also participated in RPA's thought leadership initiatives and carried out research on global philanthropy for clients. She is a frequent speaker at philanthropic conferences and events.

Donzie holds a master's in journalism from Columbia University; a master's in public administration from New York University; and a BA from Barnard College at Columbia University. A dual citizen of the United States and Portugal, Donzie is fluent in English, Portuguese, French and Spanish.

**Melissa A Berman**
President and CEO, Rockefeller Philanthropy Advisors
mberman@rockpa.org

Melissa Berman is the founding president and CEO of RPA, an innovative non-profit philanthropy service launched by the Rockefeller family in 2002. RPA's mission is to help donors create thoughtful, effective philanthropy throughout the world. RPA develops strategic plans; conducts research; manages foundations and trusts; structures major gifts; coordinates donor collaboratives; and provides re-granting and incubation services. It also publishes, convenes and speaks about innovations in thoughtful, effective philanthropy. RPA annually manages or facilitates over $400 million in giving to more than 25 countries. It has full-time staff across the United States as well as in Europe and Africa. Melissa is also an adjunct professor at Columbia Business School, a trustee of Candid and an advisory council member for the Marshall Institute at the London School of Economics. She holds a BA from Harvard University and a PhD from Stanford University.

**Peter Cafferkey**
Representative, EVPA
pcafferkey@evpa.eu.com; info@evpa.eu.com

Peter Cafferkey has been a representative of EVPA (European Venture Philanthropy Association) since 2019. EVPA has, for over 15 years, been the home for Investors *for* Impact in Europe. Now numbering over 300 members from 30 countries, the network continues to support knowledge sharing and collaboration to drive forward innovative social solutions.

In addition, since 2016, Peter has been the CEO and founder of Boncerto – a social good consultancy providing guidance and support to families looking to engage in the next generation of philanthropy and impact investing.

Peter has worked in the philanthropic and impact investing space for over 15 years, holding a number of philanthropic advisory roles with US, European and Asian foci. Peter is a regular contributor and speaker on impact investment and philanthropy around the world.

**Diana Chambers**
President, The Chambers Group Sàrl
diana@dianachambers.com

Diana Chambers is a highly respected family wealth mentor and philanthropic adviser working in confidence with ultra-high-net-worth families. While living and working in the United States, she served as the fundraiser for an educational project in Bosnia during the war; directed the Servant Leadership School in Washington DC in the 1990s, preparing compassionate leadership for America's inner cities; helped to establish Friends of Health, an advocacy group for integrative medicine practices; and then supported the Chopra Foundation before founding the Chambers Group, LLC in 2002. She has lived in Switzerland since 2014.

Diana has a deep understanding of the giving space and emphasises the importance of dialogue between donors and charitable organisations, facilitating the conversations that are vital to fulfilling relationships and successful philanthropy.

Known for championing the human side of money, Diana offers the essence of her work in her book, *True Wealth: Letters on Money, Life, and Love* (Altitude Press, 2016).

**Etienne Eichenberger**
Managing partner, WISE – philanthropy advisors, Switzerland
etienne@wise.net

Etienne Eichenberger is a partner at WISE – philanthropy advisors, one of the most recognised philanthropic advisory boutiques in Europe. Since 2004, he has provided tailored advice to donors, entrepreneurs and foundations. WISE is recognised by its peers for the quality of its work and its pioneering spirit.

Etienne previously worked for the Avina Foundation and the Swiss Development Cooperation. He is also chairman of the Swiss Philanthropy Foundation and co-founder of Sustainable Finance

Geneva; and he sits on the advisory board of the Debiopharm Chair on Family Philanthropy at IMD Business School in Lausanne.

Etienne is also a co-author of *The Family Philanthropy Navigator* and a co-founder of the Foundation Board Academy in Switzerland. He is based in Geneva.

**Barbara R Hauser**
Independent family adviser
brhauser@aol.com

Barbara Hauser, a graduate of Wellesley College and the University of Pennsylvania Law School, began her career as a private client lawyer, based in Minnesota, United States. Work for her clients included a variety of trusts and charitable structures. As the clients were successful entrepreneurs, they favoured creating their own private (charitable) foundations, despite the heavy tax regulation. She also represented a major art institute and participated in an international panel on estate planning for art. She was appointed a commissioner for the National Endowment for the Humanities and served on several boards of art institutes, theatres and health organisations. She has always enjoyed helping clients with their philanthropic objectives.

**Eileen R Heisman**
President and CEO, National Philanthropic Trust
npt@nptrust.org

Eileen R Heisman, advanced certified fundraising executive, is president and CEO of National Philanthropic Trust (NPT), the largest national independent public charity that manages donor-advised funds. Since its founding in 1996, under Eileen's leadership, NPT has raised billions in charitable assets and expanded globally, creating two new charities: NPT UK and NPT Transatlantic.

Eileen is an internationally recognised expert on philanthropy and charitable giving, advising current and future philanthropists individually and in the media, including Bloomberg News and *The Wall Street Journal*. Eileen has authored the *Donor-Advised Fund Report*, the sector's authority on donor-advised fund philanthropy, since its inception in 2007.

Eileen teaches a graduate course in philanthropy at the University of Pennsylvania's School of Social Policy and Practice, and is both a lecturer and a member of the national advisory board at the University of Michigan School of Social Work. She also serves on Carnegie Mellon University's Dietrich College board of advisers.

**Renee Karibi-Whyte**
Vice president and assistant corporate secretary, Rockefeller Philanthropy Advisors
rkaribi-whyte@rockpa.org

Renee Karibi-Whyte leads RPA's efforts to share its research and expertise on impactful philanthropic practice with individuals, families and organisations seeking to accelerate social change. As a member of the executive team and head of communications and partnerships, she is a lead contributor to RPA's Theory of the Foundation initiative, Strategic Time Horizon research, Philanthropy Roadmap guides and other knowledge-based projects that help clients and the sector to create more thoughtful, effective philanthropy. She works closely with RPA's client services teams on convenings, speaking engagements, presentations, partnerships and communications globally. Renee also leads RPA's internal and external communications strategy; manages and stewards RPA's brand; and oversees public relations. She has a law degree from Harvard Law School and a bachelor's degree from Florida A&M University.

**Ineke A Koele**
Founder, Koele Tax & Legal Perspecta
ineke@koeletaxlegal.com

Ineke Koele is an internationally renowned dual-qualified lawyer and founder of Koele Tax & Legal Perspecta, a tax boutique serving private clients and non-profits in the Netherlands. With three decades of experience and strong interpersonal skills, her practice has developed into long-term dynastic and sustainable planning for international families and innovative non-profits. Ineke's PhD focused on an international comparative study on tax and legal systems for philanthropy (IBFD, 2007).

Ineke specialises in estate law, foundations law and tax law. She regularly writes and lectures in both domestic and international forums and publications, and is a fellow of the American College of Trust and Estate Counsel and the International Academy of Trust and Estate Law. She has been ranked in Band 1 in the *Chambers High Net Worth* guide since 2019, with *Chambers* stating: "She is establishing a strong name, has a lot of energy and a very good reputation." In 2021 Ineke also won the Silver IGC award for the Global Advisor of the Year in the category Succession Planning/Trusts.

**Małgorzata Kurak**
Postdoctoral research fellow, Debiopharm Chair for Family Philanthropy, IMD Business School
malgorzata.kurak@imd.org

Małgorzata Kurak conducts research on family firm governance and management practices that allow family owners and managers to translate their larger vision into workable strategies and explore their relation to philanthropy, performance and innovation.

Małgorzata has extensive research, business and teaching experience gained as a visiting fellow at leading European think-tank Bruegel; a visiting fellow at the University of Groningen; and a teaching assistant at ESADE Business School. She is an alumna of the Global Shapers Community at the World Economic Forum and of Rotaract Wroclaw; and she served as a mentor for socially driven start-ups at the 2020-21 MassChallenge Switzerland. She earned her PhD in economics, management and organisation from *Universitat Autònoma de Barcelona* in Spain.

Małgorzata has published in numerous practitioner-oriented outlets on topics such as family philanthropy, cohesive giving, blockchain and data management in philanthropy. More recently, she co-authored a book entitled *The Family Philanthropy Navigator.*

**James Maloney**
Partner, Farrer & Co
james.maloney@farrer.co.uk

James Maloney is a partner at Farrer & Co. He qualified as a solicitor in 2005 and, following qualification, was seconded to the Science Museum in London. He advises a broad spectrum of charities and those who fund, work with and regulate them. He has particular experience of advising philanthropists on the legal aspects of structuring their giving. He advises individuals and families on the formation of charities and alternatives; donor tax reliefs; charity governance; regulatory requirements; and complex cross-border issues.

James currently serves as the deputy chair of the STEP Philanthropy Advisors Global Special Interest Group Steering Committee. He lectures on charity and law and charity tax law at Bayes Business School (formerly Cass Business School), and regularly writes and speaks on legal issues affecting the sector. He is a member of the Charity Law Association and a trustee of the Irene Taylor Trust.

**Tanja Schienke-Ohletz**
Partner, Flick Gocke Schaumburg Partnerschaft mbB
tanja.schienke@fgs.de

Tanja Schienke-Ohletz is a partner at Flick Gocke Schaumburg in Frankfurt, Germany, where she has worked since 2007. She specialises in assisting clients with national and international estate tax planning. Her clients are predominantly high-net-worth individuals, but also trustees and family companies or family offices. She often deals with clients who are interested in charitable activities, especially the establishment of German foundations, or individuals who need to structure their art collections for the next generation. She also advises German non-profit organisations, either on taxation issues or on national and international engagement.

Tanja is a frequent speaker at conferences on a wide variety of topics affecting the private client space, such as international estate planning and non-profit organisations. She also writes regularly for various legal publications specialising in trust and estate matters and non-profit organisations.

**Vanessa L Schrum**
Partner, Appleby (Bermuda) Limited
vlschrum@applebyglobal.com

Vanessa Schrum is a partner and group head of the private client and trusts practice group at Appleby (Bermuda) Limited. She first qualified as a solicitor in the United Kingdom and is admitted to the bars of Bermuda and the British Virgin Islands.

Vanessa advises on a wide range of trust and estate planning matters, including Bermuda private and commercial trust structures, private trust companies, charities, wills and the administration of estates.

Vanessa serves as a director of private and licensed trust companies and as a protector. She is a member of STEP, the International Tax Planning Association and the Bermuda Trusts Law Reform Committee; and she sits on the editorial board of *The International Family Offices Journal*.

Vanessa is a *Legal 500* Leading Individual and is also recognised in the *Chambers Global 2021 High Net Worth Guide* in Band 1; the *Citywealth* Leaders List; the *Citywealth* IFC Powerwomen Top 100 List 2019; the *Private Client Global Elite Directory*; and *Expert Guide*'s Women in Business Law.

**Peter Vogel**
Professor of family business and entrepreneurship, director of the Global Family Business Center and Debiopharm Chair for Family Philanthropy, IMD Business School
peter.vogel@imd.org

Peter Vogel is professor of family business and entrepreneurship and holder of the Debiopharm Chair for Family Philanthropy at IMD Business School in Lausanne. He is also the director of the IMD Global Family Business Center and the Global Family Business Award.

Peter works with families, owners, board members and executive teams of family enterprises and family offices globally. The focus of his work is on major organisational and governance transformations.

Peter has published in academic journals and has authored books, and is frequently referenced by leading newspapers and other media outlets around the world. He is a sought-after keynote speaker at global conferences.

Peter is the founder and chairman of Delta Venture Partners AG and is an associate partner of the Cambridge Family Enterprise Group. He is featured in the Top 100 Family Influencers globally by Family Capital.

**Christian von Oertzen**
Partner, Flick Gocke Schaumburg Partnerschaft mbB
christian.von-oertzen@fgs.de

Christian von Oertzen is a partner at Flick Gocke Schaumburg and head of the private client department. He is situated in the Frankfurt office. He has more than 25 years' experience of advising national and international clients on estate planning, probate, income tax and capital gains tax matters and charitable giving, as well as on immigration to or expatriation from Germany.

Christian lectures regularly on these legal and tax issues, and has published several manuals and articles on estate and capital gains tax planning, conflict of law questions, exit taxation and charitable organisations. He is a member of several prestigious professional institutions, including the International Academy of Estate and Trust Law, STEP and the American College of Estate and Trust Counsel.

# About Globe Law and Business

Globe Law and Business was established in 2005. From the very beginning, we set out to create law books which are sufficiently high level to be of real use to the experienced professional, yet still accessible and easy to navigate. Most of our authors are drawn from Magic Circle and other top commercial firms, both in the UK and internationally.

Our titles are carefully produced, with the utmost attention paid to editorial, design and production processes. We hope this results in high-quality publications that are easy to read, and a pleasure to own. Our titles are also available as ebooks, which are compatible with most desktop, laptop and tablet devices. In 2018 we expanded our portfolio to include journals and Special Reports, available both digitally and in hard copy format, and produced to the same high standards as our books.

In the spring of 2021, we were very pleased to announce the start of a new chapter for Globe Law and Business following the acquisition of law books under the imprint Ark Publishing. We are very much looking forward to working with our new Ark authors, many of whom are well known to us, and to further developing the law firm management list, among other areas.

We'd very much like to hear from you with your thoughts and ideas for improving what we offer. Please do feel free to email me at sian@globelawandbusiness.com with your views.

**Sian O'Neill**
Managing director
Globe Law and Business
www.globelawandbusiness.com